Ancient Japan

An Enthralling Overview of Ancient Japanese History, Starting from the Jomon Period to the Heian Period

Free limited time bonus

Stop for a moment. We have a free bonus set up for you. The problem is this: we forget 90% of everything that we read after 7 days. Crazy fact, right? Here's the solution: we've created a printable, 1-page pdf summary for this book that you're reading now. All you have to do to get your free pdf summary is to go to the following website: **https://livetolearn.lpages.co/enthrallinghistory/**

Once you do, it will be intuitive. Enjoy, and thank you!

We forget 90% of everything that we've read in 7 days...

Get the free printable pdf summary of the book you've read AND much, much more... shhhh...

Enter Your Most Frequently Used Email to Get Started

DOWNLOAD FREE PDF SUMMARY

© Enthralling History

Contents

Introduction

What is not to like about the wonderful land of the rising sun? Ask a person who has just returned from visiting Japan about the things they like most, and their answers might be the unique Japanese culture, the wondrous buildings that were built many centuries ago, the pleasant weather (especially during spring when the Sakura start to bloom), or even the unbelievable cleanliness of the Japanese cities. To put it simply, words are not enough to describe Japan.

Today, Japan is home to over 125 million people. Many people claim that their advanced technologies are astounding and that their culture is definitely one of a kind. The world's first bullet train, Tōkaidō Shinkansen, for instance, is one of the most impressive inventions that originated in Japan; believe it or not, it takes slightly over three hours to travel from the capital city of Tokyo to Osaka, which is located more than 500 kilometers (310 miles) away. This 20th-century invention alone proved the nation's excellence in the world of technology. Meanwhile, sumo matches, calming traditional tea ceremonies, Shinto rituals, geisha, and kabuki theaters are some of the things that easily distinguish Japanese culture from the rest of the world. But has Japan always been this way? When did the archipelago first witness the birth of the Japanese civilization?

To the surprise of many, back in ancient times, Japan actually developed pretty late compared to its neighboring countries on the Asian mainland. Although the first groups of humans to ever inhabit the Japanese archipelago could be traced back to prehistoric times, it was not until the 4th century BCE that Japan was first introduced to iron technology and agricultural civilization. By this time, China was in the midst of warfare and military reforms, Alexander the Great had already conquered most of the Achaemenid Empire, and the ancient Greek philosopher, Plato, had already founded his academy, which became a place of study for Aristotle. However, Japan's late start did not stop the Japanese from growing. Although the nation was initially dependent on the influences brought by the immigrants who made their way from the Asian mainland and diplomatic envoys, the people gradually thrived, reaching a turning point by the 8th century CE.

The Japanese went from living as hunter-gatherers and rice farmers who could neither write nor read into a more civilized society, especially when they transitioned into the Heian period, which began in 794 CE. The two written records of ancient Japan, *Kojiki* and *Nihon Shoki*, clearly describe the flourishing cultures of the nation. Plenty of temples were constructed, each with a touch of the unique Japanese architecture that could not be seen anywhere else.

Of course, behind all of those great developments lay a great number of conflicts. Like many other nations in the world, ancient Japan had its fair share of vicious wars, battles, and assassinations. There were cases where imperial princes planned a coup to exterminate a ruling clan leader, a surprise siege laid upon the imperial castle late at night, and, not to forget, the birth of the samurai clans and their bloody skirmishes with each other.

With that said, this book wishes not only to provide readers with a captivating insight into the colorful culture of Japan and its origin but also the important incidents and conflicts that occurred throughout the centuries that shaped the nation into what it is today. Starting from the prehistoric period where the archipelago first welcomed its first inhabitants, readers will then journey through the ancient Jomon and Yayoi period before moving on to take a glimpse at the elaborate lives of the Japanese nobles in the Nara period and the early samurai warriors who made their first appearances in the 10th century CE.

Chapter 1 – Life in the Jomon Period

Certain people believed that the entire world was shaped by the hands of either mythical or celestial beings. The ancient Greeks suggested that the universe started off in the form of nothingness that they called Chaos, while the Norse people had almost the same belief except that they referred to the void as Ginnungagap. From these empty voids came primordial beings and, later on, the universe, skies, stars, the sun, the moon, clouds, mountains, islands, and so much else. But the Greeks and Norse people are not the only ones with myths about the beginnings of their worlds; the ancient Japanese people also believed that their lands were created by powerful mythical beings.

The Creation of the Japanese Islands

Izanami and Izanagi are a pair of gods often associated by the Japanese as the creators of their archipelago. It was said that it all started when the two celestial beings were walking along a bridge floating high up in the sky that connected heaven and earth. Staring down at the great ocean, where only nothingness could be seen, the two gods began to ponder on how to transform Chaos into a world of their own. Still focusing on the nothingness below them, the gods decided to make use of their jeweled spear known as Amenonuhoko, which was gifted to them by the elder gods. With the spear, the gods stirred the deep sea, and when they lifted it up, a small droplet at the end of the spear fell into the great ocean, thus creating the very first island of Japan. This mythical island is known as Onogoroshima.

Izanagi and Izanami creating the islands of Japan.
https://commons.wikimedia.org/wiki/File:Kobayashi_Izanami_and_Izanagi.jpg

With the creation of Onogoroshima, the celestial pair finally had a land they could call home. Here, they built a legendary pillar, also known as the Heavenly August Pillar, which they later used in their rituals to start producing offspring. However, the gods started off on the wrong foot during the first ritual, which resulted in their first two children being born in the most twisted way possible. One of them was born without a single bone, almost resembling a leech. Disappointed, Izanami and Izanagi journeyed back to heaven, where they sought solutions for their misfortune from the elder gods.

Once the celestial pair had gotten the answers they needed, they traveled back to the island and performed the ritual again, correctly this time around. With the ritual a success, the two gods soon gave birth to many divine children, including the eight principal islands of Japan: Awaji, Shikoku, Oki, Tsukushi (later known as Kyushu), Iki, Tsu, Sado, and Oyamato.

How Japan Was Shaped

In contrast to the mythical legend of how the Japanese islands were shaped, science has suggested that Japan was initially attached to the eastern coast of the Eurasian continent. This was, however, over twenty million years ago. So, how did Japan get separated from the continent and transformed into a chain of islands?

Imagine our earth's continents as pieces of a jigsaw puzzle that could be attached and separated from each other at any time. Over two hundred million years ago, all the continents were attached together perfectly, just like a completed jigsaw puzzle, forming a supercontinent called Pangea. Fast forward to about fifty million years later, these continents began to drift apart, resulting in the positions we know today.

Thanks to the theory of plate tectonics, we now know that the continents are constantly on the move, drifting apart from each other. The same thing happened to Japan, which was initially a part of the Eurasian continent. About twenty thousand years ago, volcanic activity caused Japan to move eastward, taking its new position on the Pacific Ring of Fire, which explains the earthquakes and tsunamis that continue to terrorize the lands today. But if Japan was detached from the Eurasian plate many years ago, when did humans first set foot on the island chain? And how did they even travel to the archipelago?

The Discovery of the Japanese Paleolithic Age

While the ancient Japanese had Izanami and Izanagi to thank for the creation of their beautiful lands, archaeologists and historians are grateful for their discoveries of the various artifacts and fossils that reveal some stories of the past. However, many years ago, none of the Japanese believed that their lands went through the Stone Age due to the lack of evidence. Archaeologists spent their days and nights digging deep in their sites, hoping to find at least one artifact that could prove Japan did have a Paleolithic period. Their effort, however, was not very fruitful, leading to them believing that the Jomon people were the first group of humans to ever live on the islands.

But things would change right after the end of World War II. Tadahiro Aizawa was the first person to ever discover Japanese Paleolithic artifacts. Much to everyone's surprise, Tadahiro was only an amateur archaeologist, and he also happened to be a natto (fermented soybean) merchant. In 1946, while he was walking along the road on his way to conduct his daily business errands in Iwajuku, the amateur archaeologist came across a small flaked stone tool made out of obsidian, half-buried in a layer of red soil. He continued searching the area and found even more fragments of stone tools, which left him puzzled. The Japanese, at that time, believed that the Jomon were the earliest group of humans to arrive on the islands.

Three years after his discovery, Tadahiro once again found a fragment of a stone artifact; this time around, it was a stone arrowhead. He finally came to the conclusion that the islands of Japan had, in fact, been inhabited by humans way earlier than what was believed. The amateur archaeologist decided to meet a professor at one of the universities in Tokyo, hoping he could enlist more help from professionals to excavate the site. His first attempt, however, was unsuccessful, as the professor was not convinced by his findings. Many were unconvinced by Tadahiro's sudden discoveries except for one archaeologist from Meiji University who decided to assist his research. From there, full-fledged excavations were conducted, and just as the amateur archaeologist expected, more artifacts surfaced, and more sites were discovered, proving that the early inhabitants of Japan had lived through the Paleolithic period.

Tadahiro was not the only archaeologist known for the discovery of the Japanese Paleolithic period. In the 1970s, another amateur archaeologist was said to have found a number of artifacts, most of them originating from the Paleolithic period. His name was Fujimura Shinichi, and due to his remarkable discoveries at various sites, he was nicknamed the "Divine Hand." Although many other professional archaeologists were skeptical of his many findings, Fujimura's career flourished to the point where he held a position as a deputy director of the Tohoku Paleolithic Institute.

However, his success began to plummet when it was discovered that most of his findings were fraudulent. The archaeologist was caught red-handed when journalists from a newspaper managed to record footage of Fujimura planting fake artifacts at excavation sites. When the footage came to light, the archaeologist was forced to confess.

Nevertheless, through the artifacts discovered by other archaeologists—from those found by Tadahiro back in the 1940s to more recent ones—professionals have concluded that the Japanese archipelago first received inhabitants approximately forty thousand years ago. During this time, the world was at the peak of the Ice Age. Due to the sea level being 150 meters lower than what we see today, the Japanese archipelago was not 100 percent detached from the Asian continent; land bridges would have connected the islands with the continent. Since there were land bridges, humans could migrate to Japan without having to cross the sea.

It is plausible that the first humans to travel to the archipelago were following the migrations of animal herds, such as the

Naumann's elephant and the giant elk. (Some claimed the first humans came from Southeast Asia based on skeletal analyses, while others suggest Northeast Asia.) Wild animals played a big role in the early humans' lives. Most of the time, their food depended on hunting. The Naumann's elephant (an extinct species of ancient elephant), for instance, weighed between four to five tons, and its meat could feed an entire settlement for a very long time. Because of that, these elephants became an attractive hunting target, which could be the reason humans decided to follow their migration over the land bridges. The discovery of the extinct elephant's fossils in Lake Nojiri further supports this theory.

The Lifestyle of the Paleolithic Japanese

Handless stone axes.
https://commons.wikimedia.org/wiki/File:JapanesePolishedStoneAxes.JPG

The Japanese Paleolithic period, also referred to as the Pre-ceramic era, was said to have taken place nearly forty thousand years ago and lasted until the end of the Ice Age. Not much is known about the lives of these ancient people except that they were big-game hunters and gatherers. When they were not out in the wilds hunting for animals or fishing, they spent their days foraging forests, collecting nuts and berries to add to their food supplies. Various tools were found by archaeologists. One of them was the handless ax, which was possibly used to chop wood. They found a spearhead that was attached to driftwood, which would have been used for hunting, and a stone knife used to skin animals.

Since hunting was their main source of food, it is unsurprising to discover that these people moved from one place to another. They only occupied a specific location for a few weeks or months before they moved to another area, possibly following herds of animals. While some suggested that they took shelter in simple tents made out of animal skins, there are others who claimed that these people dwelled in caves, possibly in groups of ten or so. This is due to the discovery of Yamashita-Dojin, a limestone cave where the fossils of an eight-year-old prehistoric human were found. The remains were estimated to be approximately thirty-two thousand years old. Archaeologists also managed to excavate impressive fossils in a stone quarry located in Okinawa. This discovery of complete skeletons with skulls, feet, and hands received worldwide recognition. They are named Minatogawa people, and they are estimated to be seventeen thousand years old.

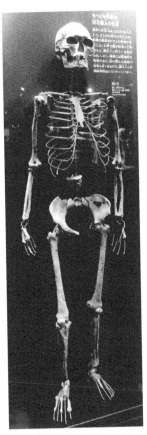

Fossil of the Minatogawa Man.
Photaro, CC BY-SA 3.0 https://creativecommons.org/licenses/by-sa/3.0 via Wikimedia Commons: https://commons.wikimedia.org/wiki/File:Fossil_of_Minatogawa_Man.jpg

The Paleolithic age soon became a thing of the past, as the people in the Japanese archipelago experienced a gradual change in both their surroundings and lifestyle. Approximately twenty thousand years ago, warmth began to replace the earth's cold climate. Later on, the glaciers began to melt, and the sea level rose, marking the end of the Ice Age. This was also when Japan was completely separated from the Asian mainland. The gradual change in the climate affected a few beings. The number of large animals, especially the Naumann's elephant and the giant elk, began to drop. Without these massive animals to hunt, the people in Japan began to modify their tools and hunting weapons. Although the tools were smaller, they remained useful.

The era following the Japanese Paleolithic age is known as the Jomon period. When these people transitioned into this new period remains debatable. Some historians believe that the Jomon period began at least twelve thousand years ago, while there are others who claim that it started as early as sixteen thousand years ago when the land bridges still existed. The word Jomon is simply translated as "cord-markings" and is named after the unique characteristics of the pottery found during this period. The Jomon period lasted for nearly ten thousand years, and it is divided into six different phases: the Incipient phase (10,500–8000 BCE), the Initial Jomon (8000–5000 BCE), Early Jomon (5000–2500 BCE), Middle Jomon (2500–1500 BCE), Late Jomon (1500–1000 BCE), and Final Jomon (1000 BCE–300 BCE).

The Incipient Phase and Initial Jomon

The Incipient phase, which took place as early as 10,500 BCE, is often categorized as the transitional phase where the Jomon people were starting to change their way of life to better suit the climate change and their surroundings. Aside from living in simple surface dwellings, the early Jomon people were believed to be hunter-gatherers.

With the end of the Ice Age, the archipelago's vegetation faced some great transformations. The southwestern region of Honshu, Shikoku, and Kyushu saw the growth of broadleaf evergreen trees filling up every corner of the lush forests. Several different tree species, such as buckeyes, chestnuts, oaks, and beeches, began to prosper, making nut-gathering activities possible. Those who took shelter in the northeastern part of these regions focused on fishing activities to sustain their families. Salmon and various shellfish were their main sources of food, while sika deer and wild boars were also hunted for their meat.

Incipient Jomon pottery.

Pottery first emerged during these two phases of the Jomon period. They were mostly used as cooking containers, and pottery with pointed bottoms was a common sight. Each of these containers featured unique cord markings, which were normally carved using sticks and sometimes shells. Flat-bottomed pots also existed, which were typically used to boil food.

Early Jomon

The Early Jomon period was when the population of the Japanese archipelago began to flourish, growing from 20,000 to approximately 100,000 people. With the growth of the population, bigger villages started to emerge across the lands. Their shelters developed from simple surface dwellings into much sturdier structures. They lived in pit houses that could fit up to five people at once. Supported by wooden pillars, the pit houses were usually built surrounding a fireplace. Villages established by the sea depended mostly on fishing, while those who lived farther inland resorted to hunting and gathering activities.

A Japanese pit house at Dōnosora site, Gifu prefecture, Japan.
Alpsdake, CC BY-SA 4.0 https://creativecommons.org/licenses/by-sa/4.0 via Wikimedia Commons: https://commons.wikimedia.org/wiki/File:Pit-house_of_D%C5%8Dnosora_site.JPG

Cord-marked cooking containers continued to be used by the Jomon people, except the pottery had more intricate patterns and shapes. Narrow-necked jars, shallow bowls, and deep storage vessels were common, while bone needles and woven baskets were created for daily use. Pottery in the shape of animals and human figurines also emerged during this phase.

Middle Jomon

As the years passed, the Japanese archipelago welcomed yet another phase of the Jomon period. During the Middle Jomon, the population of the Japanese lands continued to increase greatly, leading to the establishment of bigger villages. Pit houses were widely used; some even featured paved stone floors. The rise in the temperature, however, caused many of the communities to move to mountainous regions. Hunting, fishing, and foraging were still their main activities for food. Rabbits, ducks, deer, and bears were common targets for hunters, while gatherers would often spend their time collecting different types of berries, mushrooms, and nuts. Some historians even claimed that the earliest plant cultivation might have happened during this phase, although it was most likely uncommon.

The Jomon people also began to bury their deceased in shell mounds, with various ritualistic practices slowly emerging within their communities. While their pottery continued to evolve into more sophisticated designs, human figurines became even more common. Archaeologists suggest that they were probably used in ritualistic ceremonies.

Late Jomon

The Jomon people once again moved their villages to another location due to climate change. With the temperature drop, these people chose to settle in an area closer to the sea; most of them would often live somewhere along Honshu's eastern shores. Because of this, the Late Jomon period witnessed an explosion of fishing activities, which resulted in new fishing tools and technology. Deep-sea fishing techniques were introduced, and the creation of a toggle harpoon, an ancient fishing tool, made it possible for the Jomon people to fish larger marine animals. By this time, whales and seals had become a part of their diet.

The discovery of circular ritualistic sites filled with a number of intricate figurines and assembled stones also suggests that the Jomon people held strong beliefs. It could be plausible that they had begun believing in a number of spirits and magic. Their ceremonial sites would often feature a sophisticated female figurine, which could have been used to symbolize the goddess of earth or fertility. Their beliefs, however, varied, depending on the many tribes and communities scattered throughout the archipelago.

Final Jomon

While the population of the Jomon thrived, especially by 5000 BCE, a climate change that occurred by 1000 BCE caused their population to decline drastically. The shortage of food supplies and other environmental issues might also have played a role in this sudden decline.

However, during this period, the Japanese archipelago began to receive contacts from the Asian mainland, particularly the Korean Peninsula. By 900 BCE, settlements influenced by the Koreans started to emerge around the western region of Kyushu. Pottery styles similar to those from the peninsula were also introduced. Not only did these settlers from the Asian mainland establish new settlements across the archipelago, but they also brought precious knowledge in rice cultivation and metalworking. Later on, hunting and foraging activities slowed down as rice cultivation became more widespread. This marked the end of the Jomon period.

Chapter 2 – Art, Culture, and Transition

The earth is indeed full of mysteries. Life sprung up at least tens of thousands of years ago, but it is hard for us to imagine how the world was back then. However, thanks to the many artifacts that have survived through the years, archaeologists and scholars have managed to put the pieces together and provide us with an insight into the lives of many ancient beings. The Jomon pottery, for instance, could tell us about the daily lives of the Jomon people in great detail.

When exactly the Japanese archipelago transitioned from the Paleolithic Age to the Neolithic Jomon period is disputed, but it is safe to say that the usage of pottery is what distinguishes the two periods. The first person to ever discover the unique and ancient Japanese pottery was a 19th-century American zoologist and archaeologist named Edward S. Morse. He was also the same person responsible for naming their pottery "Jomon," which simply means cord pattern in Japanese. The origins of the pottery, however, remain debatable. Since the title of the earliest type of ceramic vessels in East Asia is given to China, it is plausible that

Jomon pottery was somehow influenced by Chinese techniques and traditions.

Since the Jomon period lasted for tens of thousands of years, scholars divided the period into different phases. Each of these phases featured different kinds of pottery, beliefs, and cultures. Some of the oldest Jomon pottery were the ones excavated from Shinonouchi, Nagano, as well as another site in Amouri called Odai-Yamamoto. These ancient artifacts can be traced back to 13,000 BCE, making them some of the oldest pottery in the world. During the early Jomon period, pottery was created in a rather simple design; they typically featured pointed bottoms, hollow bodies, and, of course, a distinctive rope pattern imprinted on the exterior surface. They were normally used as storage vessels and cooking containers.

Since a potter's wheel did not yet exist during the ancient period, the Jomon created these clay vessels using only their hands. Using the coil method, these people would shape their pottery layer by layer. Once the process of shaping the pottery was done, twines, ropes, grasses, and sometimes even seashells were imprinted on the wet clay to produce designs on the exterior surface. To finish them, the pottery had to go through a firing process, but due to the lack of a kiln, the Jomon would expose the pottery under the scorching sun before firing it in a bonfire that had a temperature no higher than 900°C (1652°F). To ensure they were waterproof, these vessels were usually covered with a lacquer made out of sap from the tree *Rhus verniciflua*.

By the Middle Jomon period, the pottery had evolved, featuring more intricate designs and shapes. Scholars divided the pottery into six different categories: *fukabachi* (deep bowls), *asabachi* (shallow bowls), *hachi* (medium-depth bowls), *sara* (plates), *tsubo* (narrow vessels with long necks), and *chuko* (spouted vessels). The pottery in the Middle Jomon evolved from pointed ends into flat bottoms, allowing them to be placed on flat surfaces easily.

An intricate Jomon flame vessel.
Cleveland Museum of Art, CC0, via Wikimedia Commons:
https://commons.wikimedia.org/wiki/File:Clevelandart_1984.68.jpg

The most famous type of Jomon pottery, called flame ware, was first introduced during this phase. Mostly found in central Honshu, these flame wares typically sport an opening wider than their base. Since they were most likely used in cooking activities, especially in boiling food, the reason behind the structure was to avoid having the contents boil over. These elaborately decorated pottery pieces were still made using the coil method and were also covered with thin rolls of clay, which were shaped into swirls, crests, and even holes. Although widely used as cooking pots, archaeologists suggest that they were also used in ritualistic ceremonies from time to time, especially in burial rites.

In the Late Jomon period, however, these highly decorated pottery pieces became less common. The Jomon people began to prioritize a vessel's functionality instead of intricate designs. Spouted pottery, round-bottomed vessels, short ceramic containers, and even incense burners began to emerge widely across the archipelago.

While the finer pottery still existed, they were only used in ritualistic practices.

Round-bottomed pottery from the Final Jomon.
https://commons.wikimedia.org/wiki/File:Jar_with_cord_marks,_Japan,_Hokkaido,_final_Jomon_period,_c._1000_BC,_earthenware,_iron-red_pigment_-_Peabody_Essex_Museum_-_DSC07531.jpg

The Final Jomon saw the birth of yet another piece of pottery that was unique to the archipelago. Dogū, which literally translates as "earthen figure," was first discovered in the 17th century. It has a rather peculiar appearance. While Dogū could be in any sort of form—be it an animal or a human—the most popular Dogū ever discovered was the one from Kamegaoka, Aomori Prefecture. Its prominent features include its coffee bean-shaped eyes, tiny nose and mouth, and an elaborate crown placed on its oval head. The size of these figurines varies; some measure at least forty centimeters (about sixteen inches) tall, while others stand at one meter (about three feet). The Dogū was often painted in red pigments and featured a complex detail on its body that perhaps indicated tattoos, scarring, body paint, or jewelry.

Dogū excavated from Ebisuda Site in Tajiri, Miyagi Prefecture, Japan.
World Imaging, CC BY-SA 3.0 https://creativecommons.org/licenses/by-sa/3.0 via Wikimedia Commons: https://commons.wikimedia.org/wiki/File:Dogu_Miyagi_1000_BCE_400_BCE.jpg

The purpose of this clay figurine, however, is not clear. Some claim that it was once used as a talisman for good health and safe childbirth, while others suggest that it was an item of worship the Jomon people prayed to in order to be blessed with an abundance of food. It might have also been used as an offering for a specific goddess and spirit. It is even possible that it was not to religious practice at all and was merely used as a children's toy. Nevertheless, the discovery of the Dogū is indeed valuable since it tells us of how expressive and creative the Jomon people were, despite the lack of advanced tools and technology.

The Beliefs of the Jomon People

The increasing number of figurines, stone circles, rods, and other ritualistic objects created during the Late and Final Jomon suggest that these ancient people had already established their own beliefs and religious practices. Although we cannot be sure what kind of ritualistic ceremonies the Jomon people participated in, it is likely that most of them were performed to commemorate or celebrate bountiful hunting catches and harvests. Archaeologists also managed to excavate pit houses that were filled with an array of clay figurines, ritual masks, highly decorated vessels, and even phallic stones, which might indicate that they belonged to shamans who were responsible for leading religious ceremonies.

Late Jomon clay head, possibly used in ritualistic ceremonies.
PHGCOM, CC BY-SA 3.0 https://creativecommons.org/licenses/by-sa/3.0 via Wikimedia Commons: https://commons.wikimedia.org/wiki/File:Late_Jomon_clay_head_Shidanai_Iwateken_1.500BCE_100 0BCE.jpg

Animism beliefs and animal worship might have also been practiced by the Jomon people. Pottery featuring animal motifs, especially snakes, were found around the Yatsugatake Mountains in Nagano Prefecture. Due to the discovery of this pottery, experts arrived at the conclusion that certain tribes of the Jomon people— mostly those who lived within the mountains and coastal areas—were part of snake cults. They might have practiced certain rituals presided over by female shamans. It is possible that the snake motifs carved onto the clay pottery were depictions of the mamushi or Japanese pit viper, the most venomous snake in Japan. However, snakes were not the only animals to be depicted on their pottery, as archaeologists have also discovered clay figurines that resembled rodents.

Some of the clay figurines even came with highly complex details on their body, face, and arms, which led scholars to believe that the Jomon people were familiar with tattoos. Some suggest that they actually tattooed themselves on both their bodies and faces. In fact, the Ainu people, who are believed to share the same DNA as the Jomon people, were known for their tattoos, although the tradition of tattooing body parts and faces was mainly for women.

An Ainu woman with a facial tattoo.
https://commons.wikimedia.org/wiki/File:Ainu_woman_(from_a_book_Published_in_193 1)_P.81.png

The discovery of Jomon skulls with missing teeth also indicates that they might have practiced tooth ablation, a ritualistic practice that involves the removal of a person's healthy teeth. This ritual first took place during the Late Jomon period, and it was even practiced by some of the Yayoi people. To the Jomon people, tooth ablation was considered crucial since their altered look signified their status and age; the sets of teeth extracted from a person who had just reached puberty differed from those who had just been married. There were also cases where tooth ablation was done after the death of a loved one, either one's parents or spouse.

Burial Rites of the Jomon People

Of course, there are no intricate details about what happened when death occurred within a tribe or village. But with the discovery of the many stone circles, along with other ritualistic tools that indicate the strong beliefs of these ancient people in spirits and magic, it is safe to assume that a particular ritual or ceremony must have taken place to honor the dead. It is possible that they also buried animals, especially dogs, which were sometimes kept as pets.

Early on, the dead would be buried in shell mounds with their legs folded close to their chest, but as the years passed, the Jomon began using burial pits and jars. The latter were commonly used to bury children, infants, and unborn fetuses. Burial sites were normally placed at the center of a village, with most of them featuring grave markers. Archaeologists suggest that these ancient people had a particular way of marking the graves of their loved ones; they would place stones in a circular arrangement known as *kanjo-haiseki-bo*. Cremations also existed during this era, but they were rarely practiced. In some cases, the body of the deceased would be buried underneath the floor of their pit dwelling. Some also suggest that the body was placed directly on the floor before being covered with shell layers. Since death was considered unlucky and impure, the family members of the deceased would move out of the dwelling, abandoning it entirely.

Children might have had a special place in the hearts of the Jomon people since they took great care when it came to burying their lifeless bodies. Instead of being buried the same way as the adults, deceased children, infants, and unborn fetuses had their own burial tradition. They were buried in a curled-up position in burial jars made out of clay. Although some adults were buried in burial jars, by the starting of the Final Jomon period, this method was commonly used for infants, especially those who had died at the age of thirty-eight weeks or so. The Sanai Maruyama site alone had nearly eight hundred burial jars that contained the remains of children and infants.

At the start of this ancient period, the Jomon people would often bury their dead along with common items typically used in their daily lives. This included things like stone tools, arrowheads, and simple clay vessels. However, by the beginning of the Middle Jomon, their burial customs began to evolve, with the people burying their dead with an abundance of more elaborate items, such as ornaments and jewelry like shell bracelets, stone and shark tooth pendants, earrings, and jade beads. Ritualistic items, such as complex pottery vessels, figurines, clay tablets, and stone rods, were also included in graves, suggesting that these people probably believed in life after death.

Chapter 3 – The Yayoi Period

It is plausible that the Jomon period ended by the 3rd century BCE when its population plummeted and food sources were scarce due to their diet being fully dependent on hunting and foraging. Soon, another group of people arrived in the land of the rising sun, and they brought useful knowledge of rice cultivation and metalworking with them. We could say that Japan developed pretty late compared to other parts of the world. In the 3rd century BCE, China was constructing the Great Wall. Ancient Egypt had just finished building the Lighthouse of Alexandria. Nevertheless, on the islands of Japan, the 3rd century BCE marks the start of the Yayoi period, which lasted for at least five to six centuries. Unlike the word Jomon, which was named after the period's pottery style, Yayoi was named after a district in Tokyo. Here, the first artifacts originating from this period were discovered back in the 19th century.

The Origins of the Yayoi People

Many studies have been conducted to determine whether or not the Yayoi people were related to those from the Jomon period. The skull shapes of these two people groups were analyzed and compared, and their DNA was extracted for research. It was then revealed that there were, indeed, distinct differences between the two groups of people. While the Jomon people shared a little in common with the modern Japanese—although they did have some small similarities with the indigenous Ainu—the Yayoi people were the ones believed to be directly linked to the modern Japanese. But unearthing the roots of the Japanese is far more complicated than one might expect since there are many conflicting theories. In fact, no one is even sure what happened to the Jomon people after the Yayois' arrival. Were they violently replaced, or was there any intermarriage between the two groups?

Although where the Yayoi people came from remains a topic of debate today, scholars, historians, and archaeologists alike suggested that it involved migrations of people from either the Korean Peninsula via the Tsushima Strait or northern China across the Yellow Sea. Since the land bridges that connected Japan to the Asian continent had already been submerged due to the rising sea, it is safe to assume that sea-faring migrations were involved. The Yayoi culture was also said to first emerge in Kyushu, and in just a blink of an eye, it spread to the other part of the archipelago, first to the east and then up north.

Since the origin of wet rice farming can be traced back to China's Yangtze River, it could also be possible that the Yayoi people were initially farmers from this area who decided to migrate to the archipelago. To test this theory, research was carried out by Satoshi Yamaguchi, a researcher from Japan's National Museum of Nature and Science. The remains of the Yayoi people discovered in two Japanese prefectures, Yamaguchi and Fukuoka, were thoroughly examined and compared with the remains from Jiangsu, a Chinese province. At the end of the three-year research, they found that the remains bore many similarities, especially in their skulls and limbs.

The Legend of Xu Fu

Other than migrations of rice farmers from the Asian continent, some of the Japanese also believed that the advanced techniques of farming were actually brought into their lands by Xu Fu, who also introduced the knowledge of traditional medicines to the native on the islands.

Xu Fu, also called Jofuku by the Japanese, was an alchemist who called the ancient Chinese state of Qi his homeland. The alchemist served Qin Shi Huang, the founder and first emperor of the Qin dynasty, as a court sorcerer. Since Xu Fu was an alchemist and an explorer, it is not surprising to learn that Xu Fu held much knowledge. He somehow learned that there were three celestial islands in the world where their inhabitants were all immortals. These lands were named Penglai, Fangzhang, and Yingzhou. The immortals were said to be thousands of years old, and they lived in a gold palace nestled within the mountains. On the island of Penglai, one could feast night and day without having to worry about their bowls getting empty. The enchanted fruits growing in the area could also grant eternal youth.

And so, when the emperor—who was famously known to have an obsession with immortality— learned about the existence of these magical lands, he ordered the alchemist to set sail and search for the key to immortality: the elixir of life. Some say the emperor's obsession with immortality had to do with his extreme fear of death, especially since so many people wanted to spill his blood. In fact, he was believed to have survived two murder attempts. Another reason could also be the ominous message Qin Shi Huang saw on a meteor that hit Dongjun back in 211 BCE. The message stated that he would soon die and that all of his lands would be divided, which somehow came true since the emperor died in 210 BCE after possibly consuming an elixir containing mercury prepared by his own court alchemists and physicians. To make matters worse, the Qin dynasty collapsed about five years after his death, and his lands were, indeed, divided.

Xu Fu set sail under the order of his emperor and began his expedition across the East Sea in search of the celestial island. The alchemist brought along a few thousand men, women, and children.

The expedition, however, was nothing but a waste of time, as Xu Fu never found any islands or mountains of the immortals. And so, he set sail back to his homeland. When questioned by the emperor about his adventure and whether he had gotten the elixir of life, Xu Fu answered that he was forced to retreat, as there was a massive sea creature underneath the deep sea patiently waiting to attack his ship. Upon hearing the alchemist's explanation, the emperor sent highly skilled archers to the sea, where they killed the creature believed to be blocking Xu Fu's way.

Xu Fu's expedition for the elixir of immortality.
https://commons.wikimedia.org/wiki/File:Xu_Fu_expedition%27s_for_the_elixir_of_life.jpg

With the creature gone, the emperor again sent Xu Fu across the ocean to retrieve the magical elixir. This time around, Xu Fu had a total of three thousand men, women, and children on board, along with many provisions, seeds, and silks. However, just as last time, Xu Fu never found Penglai. He was well aware that he could never return home since the emperor would want to have his head on a plate for failing his task. So, Xu Fu never returned, and that was the last time anyone ever heard of him or his crew.

Legend has it that Xu Fu and his crew actually landed in Japan, thinking Mount Fuji to be the celestial Mount Penglai. Some believed that upon landing on the archipelago, the alchemist shared much of his knowledge with the people there. This includes the techniques of rice cultivation. The Japanese people eventually worshiped the alchemist as their god of farming; statues honoring him can be found in Japan today. Some even believe that he was the same person as Emperor Jimmu, Japan's first emperor, as recorded in the *Nihon Shoki* and *Kojiki*.

The Daily Lives of the Yayoi People

With the precious knowledge of wet rice cultivation, the Japanese archipelago became extremely valuable to the Yayoi people. Agriculture was considered their main source of food, and choosing the right land to set up a settlement was, of course, one of their highest priorities. During the early times of the Yayoi period, the people would often choose healthy lands that featured either high terraces or valleys surrounded by rolling hills and mountains. The Itatsuke site in Fukuoka Prefecture is one of the examples that had all of the above features. However, as more and more settlements were built and rice farming began to spread throughout the islands, land became more limited, and the people had no other choice but to settle on the alluvial plains.

Although the art of agriculture and metalworking were still new to these ancient Japanese, the Yayoi people had no problem with developing technologies to improve their fields. Once they had gathered enough wood, the farmers would carve and create wooden stakes, which they used to outline their rice fields. To provide a continuous water supply and irrigate the rice fields, the farmers built canals and waterways. Some settlements even went the extra mile by constructing canals right under their rice fields, thus making water recycling possible. Wells were also built in close proximity to the farming fields to ease the process of obtaining water.

Stone tools such as hoes and knives were widely used at first, probably due to the minimal supplies of iron and metal, but it did not take long for them to develop proper and sturdier tools to aid in their farming activities. Later on, the blades of their stone knives were replaced with iron, and they would use them to harvest rice. Other tools that the Yayoi people used in their daily farming activities include *geta*, a pair of wooden clogs often used to walk through marshy grounds; *eburi*, which was used to smoothen the paddy fields; and *ooashi*, a paddy field tramper. These wooden tools were first discovered by archaeologists at the Toro site in Shizuoka. Believe it or not, these useful wooden tools are still used today. The harvested rice was then gathered and stored in storage jars before being kept in underground pits or elevated wooden storehouses.

Rice was not the only thing found on the farms of the Yayoi people, although it was their main source of food. Archaeologists found a total of thirty-seven other plants cultivated on their lands, including adzuki beans, barley, foxtail millet, and gourds. Hunting activities and foraging were not completely replaced, as some of them hunted for wild animals and journeyed into the wilds every now and then. They also weaved textiles on a daily basis and tended to the wild boars that they kept in their villages.

With the introduction of agricultural activities, the population of the Japanese archipelago skyrocketed, reaching almost two million people at its peak. The Yayoi people began settling permanently and lived in bigger communities. Early on, their houses were pretty much identical to those originating from the Jomon period. Pit houses featuring thatched roofs and earthen floors were a common sight during this time. As time passed and their technology advanced, these groups of dwellings were surrounded by moats to prevent attacks. Other structures were built, such as granaries and wooden storehouses, which were typically used to store rice and other crops.

Reconstruction of a Yayoi village with an elevated granary.

Many pottery pieces were also found at various sites. While pottery in the Jomon period was known for its intricate shapes and designs, those originating from the Yayoi period are simpler; it seems the Yayoi prioritized usefulness. Long-necked storage vessels, round-mouthed cooking pots, pedestalled dishes, and serving bowls were common pottery during this period. While scholars believed that the shapes of pottery and jars might have come from Korea since they bore similarities with Mumun pottery, others suggest that Jomon influences played a role.

Religion, Beliefs, and Burial Ceremonies of the Yayoi Period

By the 1st century BCE, bronze started to be widely used by the Yayoi people. While iron and metal were commonly used to create farming tools, weapons, and armor, bronze was often smelted to make ritual items. Dōtaku, for instance, were huge bells made out of bronze. According to Japanese folklore, dōtaku were actually emergency bells that were used by the sentinels whenever they spotted a threat coming their way. Once a dōtaku was rung by the sentinels, warriors would prepare themselves to defend their settlements. However, certain scholars and historians have suggested that these bronze bells were not used to sound emergencies. Dōtaku have rather thin walls, and because of that, it would not resonate like a fully functioning bell. So, they came to the conclusion that dōtaku were, in fact, ritual items.

A bronze dōtaku.
https://commons.wikimedia.org/wiki/File:Dotaku_LACMA_M.58.9.3_(2_of_2).jpg

Most of these bronze bells were found with images of various animals, such as wild boars, dogs, birds, praying mantises, and even dragonflies, carved on the surface. But the most prominent animals featured on these bells were deer and cranes; carvings of deer were also featured on some of the Yayoi pottery. This reason alone led archaeologists to believe that the Yayoi people already had their own beliefs.

We have learned that the origins of Shintoism can be traced back to the Yayoi period. By this time, they already had shamans and priests. This fact is not at all surprising, especially since experts discovered that certain animals were considered sacred to the Yayoi people and played an important role when it came to agriculture. Farmers performed a ritual where they would sow seeds in deer blood, as they believed that deer could help improve the growth of rice. A deer's antlers are known for their rapid growth; they shed and grow new antlers every year. In spring, their antlers begin to grow and continue to develop all throughout the year until winter, when antlers are supposed to shed, repeating the entire cycle again. This cycle was believed to be connected to the growth of rice and other plants.

Apart from using blood to enhance the growth of their plants, these people would also transport the dōtaku to an isolated location away from their settlements and bury the bronze bells deep underground to receive the earth's life force. This holy rite was to ensure that their lands remained fertile.

Indeed, the Yayoi people valued their agricultural growth more than anything, but they performed rituals for other things too. It is believed that when a person died in a settlement, the entire village would enter a mourning phase that lasted for ten days. During that time, the villagers were said to dress in hemp clothes and restrict themselves from eating any sort of meat. The leader of the settlement would then wail as others participated in a ritual where they sang, danced, and drank. Once the mourning period was over, the family members of the dead would head into the waters and perform a type of purification to cleanse themselves from all the impurities of the dead.

As for the dead, their last stop would be at the burial mounds. They would be buried in wooden coffins, although some sources suggest that this method was only used during the early years of the period. Some were also buried in burial jars along with various kinds of items, such as weapons, pottery, jewelry, and ritualistic items like bronze mirrors and swords. These items were often only in the graves of those who held higher positions in a settlement.

Social Classes, Wars, and Relationship with China

Since Japan had no writing system during this period, the earliest written documents that describe the ancient Japanese are from China. These old documents are known as *Wei Shu* (*Book of Wei*) and *Han Shu* (*Book of Han*). Referring to Japan as Wa, historians from ancient China tell us that by the late Yayoi period, Japan had over one hundred different communities or states, with each one of them ruled by wealthy landowners or chieftains.

Those who possessed more metal, bronze, glass, and even silk were considered elite members of a settlement. Men with higher status were said to have many wives compared to the commoners, and those from lower classes were required to show their respect. Whenever someone with an elite status walked by, commoners had to step to the side of the road and make way for them. This was practiced by the Japanese until the 19th century CE.

As the Yayoi people strived toward civilization, they became more accustomed to war and conquest. Iron and bronze were melted, and wood was gathered to create more weapons, shields, and armor. More settlements emerged, and the land became even more limited, so these people were left with no choice but to fight each other in order to conquer fertile lands to house and support their growing population. With the increasing number of wars, the people began to fortify their settlements by digging dry moats and installing *sakamogi* or sharp wooden stakes to keep their enemies at bay. Watchtowers were built, and sentinels were stationed to keep an eye on invaders from afar.

The ancient Chinese records also mentioned that certain communities from the lands of Wa would send tribute to the Chinese emperors from time to time. In 57 CE, the state of Nu (now located on Hakata Bay, Kyushu) once sent emissaries to the emperor of the Han dynasty. In return, the emperor granted them a golden seal as a sign of a diplomatic relationship. The golden seal was lost for thousands of years, but it was later rediscovered by a farmer in 1784.

The golden seal sent by Emperor Guangwu of Han in 57 CE.
https://commons.wikimedia.org/wiki/File:King_of_Na_gold_seal.jpg

The Kingdom of Yamatai

Another decade replaced the other, and the Japanese archipelago was plagued by numerous wars and violence. Kingdoms waged wars with each other, and swords clashed no matter the time of day. However, according to the Chinese records, there was one kingdom that stood out; it was known as Yamatai. The kingdom rose to power when it successfully conquered a total of thirty states of the Japanese islands and ruled over them peacefully.

The kingdom of Yamatai was led by a shaman queen who went by the name Himiko. She was first put on the throne by her own people and was believed to possess religious powers. Some even claimed that the queen was, in fact, a direct descendant of the Shinto sun goddess, Amaterasu, while others also suggested that Himiko was the same figure as the legendary Empress Jingū.

However, only a few ever got a chance to see Himiko in person, as she resided in her palace, which was well-guarded by dozens of guards and watchmen. She was tended by a thousand female servants, and her younger brother was often the only one to meet her face to face.

Himiko never married, and she never left her palace. Since she preferred to devote herself entirely to shamanism, the queen conveyed her orders through her younger brother, who would pass them to the people of her kingdom. Under Himiko's reign, peace was possible, and more states acknowledged her as a ruler. To solidify her power, Himiko sent envoys to China with slaves and fine pieces of cloth as tributes. Noticing her influence over the lands of Wa, the Chinese Wei dynasty honored her with the title "Queen of Wa, Friendly to Wei." Along with the title and in return for her generous tributes, Himiko was gifted with a golden seal, a hundred bronze mirrors, and swords. And so, Queen Himiko became the first ruler of Japan.

Queen Himiko managed to restore peace and rule the lands of Japan for over fifty years. According to the Chinese records, Japan transformed into an organized kingdom with political stability. Law was established, and punishments were invented. The queen, however, finally passed away in 248 CE, and her remains were interred in a massive tomb, which archaeologists believed to be located in Nara Prefecture. The death of Queen Himiko also marked the end of the Yayoi period.

Chapter 4 – Shintoism

Upon looking at their first child, both Izanagi and Izanami were horrified. The child who they called Hiruko— soon known as Ebisu—was the very first kami to be born in Japan, but his appearance at birth was rather twisted. He was born without a single bone in his body, which explains why his name also meant the "Leech Child." Hiruko was later placed in a boat of reeds by his parents, who then set it adrift into the open sea. Although the kami had been born with deformities, it was said he grew a pair of legs and other limbs at the age of three. When he first washed ashore after his parents abandoned him, Hiruko was found and taken in by a group of Ainu people. He learned how to walk, talk, and smile. Soon, Hiruko went by the name Ebisu and became the patron god of fishermen as well as one of the Seven Lucky Gods or Shichifukujin.

It turns out that Ebisu's deformities were caused by none other than Izanagi and Izanami themselves. To produce offspring, the two deities participated in a ritual where they had to circle around the Heavenly August Pillar in the opposite direction. When they neared each other, Izanagi was supposed to greet his partner first; however, during their first ritual, Izanami was the one who spoke before her husband. This mistake resulted in the unfortunate birth of Hiruko.

However, the two deities managed to perform the sacred ritual correctly after consulting the elder gods in heaven, who explained what had gone wrong. With the ritual performed perfectly the second time around, Izanami gave birth to many other kami, including the eight principal islands of Japan, Watatsumi (kami of the sea), Kukunochi (kami of the trees), Oyamatsumi (kami of the mountains), and Kagutsuchi (kami of fire). Although the ritual was fruitful, resulting in the birth of many kami, Izanami had to pay a heavy price—death.

Izanami faced her fate when she gave birth to Kagutsuchi. Being the kami of fire, Kagutsuchi burned his mother to death as soon as he was delivered. Enraged, Izanagi unsheathed his legendary sword, Ameno Ohabari, and killed his son. He chopped Kagutsuchi's remains into eight pieces and scattered them throughout the islands, resulting in the eight major active volcanoes of Japan. From Kagutsuchi's blood dripping from the great sword came several more kami. The most prominent one is Takemikazuchi, the kami of thunder often associated with martial arts and believed to be the creator of sumo.

Izanagi's journey and the birth of many new kami did not stop there. Driven by extreme sadness and sorrow, Izanagi decided to venture into the underworld or Yomi, hoping to bring his wife back to the world of the living. After urging Izanami to leave the underworld and return home, Izanagi was informed that his wife had already eaten the food of the underworld, thus making her one with the land of the dead. Izanami, however, tried pleading with the gods and asked for their permission to return home with Izanagi. In the meantime, she made Izanagi promise that he would never try to look at her. Missing his beloved wife, Izanagi eventually became impatient and broke his promise by looking at her. But instead of feeling joy at seeing his long-lost wife, he was terrified, as Izanami's entire body was already decomposing and covered with wriggling maggots.

Shocked by the horrifying state of his wife, Izanagi ran away and decided to return to the world of the living without Izanami. Learning of her husband's intentions to abandon her, Izanami, along with the demons of thunder (Yakusanoikazuchi) and the ugly hags of the underworld (Yomotsu-shikome), chased after the terrified man. Luckily for Izanagi, he successfully escaped the underworld and quickly blocked the entrance to Yomi with a massive boulder, thus separating the two lands.

To cleanse himself of the underworld, Izanagi performed a ritual in the River Woto. This cleansing ritual is called *harae*, and it is one of the most important rituals in Shintoism. As Izanagi performed the purification ritual in the river, he gave birth to more kami: Amaterasu, the goddess of the sun and the mythical ancestor to Japan's emperors; Tsukuyomi, the god of the moon; and Susanoo, god of storms. These kami, along with the purification ritual, are some of the most important aspects of Shintoism.

But what exactly is Shintoism, and where did it come from? Before the arrival of Buddhism in Japan in the 6th century, its people believed in Shintoism. Shintoism was even acknowledged as the state religion back in the Meiji period. During this time, priests were appointed as state officials, and the building of shrines was put first. People would also worship their emperor since they believed that the imperial line descended from the most important kami in Shinto, Amaterasu. This, however, only lasted until the end of World War II. Today, both Shintoism and Buddhism coexist peacefully.

Although known around the globe as another type of indigenous religion, the Japanese tend not to classify Shintoism as one. Unlike other major world religions, Shintoism has neither a founder nor sacred texts like the Bible or the Quran. There is neither right nor wrong in Shintoism. Humans are believed to be born good and pure, and evil is caused by malevolent spirits.

To put it in simple words, no one knows when Shintoism exactly surfaced. But with archaeological evidence, scholars and historians believe that many of its practices began during the Yayoi period, although the earliest writing about Shintoism dates back to 712 CE. It is called *Kojiki* (*Record of Ancient Matters*). The prehistoric people, including the earliest inhabitants of Japan, were familiar with animism; they believed that everything in this world—from mountains to grasses, rocks, wild animals, places, and even the weather—possessed a spiritual essence. In Shintoism, it is believed that a spirit dwells in every single thing surrounding us.

Torii gates, a traditional Japanese gate placed at the entrance of a Shinto shrine to mark the transition from our world to a sacred site.
Balon Greyjoy, CC0, via Wikimedia Commons: Balon Greyjoy, CC0, via Wikimedia Commons:
https://commons.wikimedia.org/wiki/File:20181110_Fushimi_Inari_Torii_10.jpg

Shinto simply means the way of the kami. As the translation suggests, those who practice this two-thousand-year-old religion worship kami. But what exactly is a kami? Some might translate the word as either deities or gods, but a kami is not restricted only to godlike figures. In Shinto beliefs, kami can be anything, such as the forces of nature or the spirits of dead ancestors. The river has a kami, and so do the towering volcanoes, waterfalls, and trees growing in the middle of a lush forest. Shintoism teaches that the physical world itself is sacred and needs to be respected at all times.

Amaterasu, the Most Important Kami in Shinto

Amaterasu, whose name means the "Shining in Heaven," was born from Izanagi's left eye as he performed the purification ritual after his return from the underworld. Appointed as the ruler of the High Celestial Plain (Takamagahara) by her father, Amaterasu is also the elder sister to the mischievous yet impetuous god of storms, Susanoo. Besides being widely known as the ancestor of the imperial line of Japan, Amaterasu was also said to have taught humans how to weave cloth and plant rice. But those were not the biggest blessings that the kami bestowed upon the universe. Amaterasu was the goddess of the sun, and without the magnificent light shining out of her, both the world of humans and the heavens would plunge into total darkness, which had already happened once.

It all began when Susanoo was expelled by Izanagi when he was said to have caused nothing but nuisance upon the world. Before leaving Takamagahara, the mischievous storm god decided to meet Amaterasu at her palace just so he could bid her farewell. This event, however, turned into chaos, as the two siblings ended up in an argument. Susanoo, who was known for his temper tantrums, wreaked havoc across the celestial plain; he burned Amaterasu's rice fields, destroyed parts of her palace, and defecated on her high seat. Seeing that his sister's reaction was not what he had hoped for, Susanoo came up with more mischief. The god first flayed a beautiful spotted horse alive. Then, standing on top of the roof, Susanoo threw the flayed horse into Amaterasu's weaving hall. The poor horse fell helplessly on the floor and terrified a few of Amaterasu's sacred weaving maidens, who had peacefully been weaving clothes for the gods. More chaos ensued when one of them accidentally struck herself against a weaving shuttle and died.

Learning about the death of one of her beloved weavers, Amaterasu was overwhelmed with anger and sadness. And so, the goddess of the sun decided to leave her palace and lock herself in a cave called Ama-no-Iwato. Since she had blocked the entrance of the cave with a massive boulder, none could enter, and her shimmering light soon disappeared from the universe. With the sun gone, Takamagahara and the earth fell into darkness. Crops began to wither, food supplies deteriorated, and evil spirits started to roam the world, causing all kinds of trouble.

Realizing that the catastrophe was happening due to the absence of Amaterasu's radiant light, the kami of Takamagahara began plotting ways to persuade the goddess to leave her hiding. Omoikane, the Shinto god of wisdom, first suggested they place roosters in front of the cave, hoping that their crows would trick Amaterasu into thinking that it was finally dawn. Then, they planted a sakaki tree—a sacred evergreen in Shintoism—right in front of the cave entrance and placed a huge mirror on its trunk.

Amaterasu was puzzled when she heard the roosters crow since it was impossible for dawn to emerge without her light. Moments later, the goddess heard loud laughter coming from the many kami who had gathered in front of the cave. The laughter got louder as Amenouzume, the patron goddess of dancers, performed a wild dance on an upturned tub. One of the deities also announced that another shining goddess had arrived who was just as magnificent as the goddess of the sun herself. Finally curious, Amaterasu slowly moved the boulder blocking the cave entrance and peeked through the gap. The first thing she saw was her own radiant reflection in the sacred mirror.

Amaterasu was in complete awe, thinking the reflection was the newly arrived deity. Without delaying a single moment more, Ame-no-tajikarao, the kami known for his strong hands, yanked the sun goddess out of her hideout. The cave entrance was then sealed with Shimenawa, a straw rope, which later became an item used in Shinto purification rituals. As Amaterasu got closer to the mirror, she finally realized that she was looking at her own beautiful reflection. The goddess now knew of her important role in the universe and how wrong it was to deprive the world of her glorious light.

Amaterasu emerging out of her cave, shining the entire world with her radiant light.
https://commons.wikimedia.org/wiki/File:Amaterasu_cave.JPG

And so, with Amaterasu out of hiding, the world was blessed with her light. Crops began to prosper, the evil spirits went back to where they came from, and joy filled the air yet again.

The Story of Hōsōgami, the Kami of Smallpox

Although most of the kami worshiped by Shinto practitioners are generally good spirits who wish to see humans flourish and prosper, there are also kami associated with evil and sickness, such as Hōsōgami, the kami of smallpox. This particular kami is often depicted as an old man carrying a torn Japanese traditional fan (*uchiwa*) or small demons. This kami traveled from one village to another, spreading smallpox to the unfortunate villagers. Despite being pictured as temperamental spirits or demons, Hōsōgami were said to have some weaknesses; they are terrified of dogs and the color red. The latter was due to the color red being a symbol of good health. Because of that, villagers back then would often be seen hanging *aka-e*, a red woodblock print, in their houses. Some of these prints even feature a picture of Shōki, a mythical god said to have the ability to vanquish evil spirits and ghosts. Aside from the prints, other protective talismans include toys in the shape of dogs and red clothing.

Even though Hōsōgami brought nothing but sickness to the villagers, some also believed they could stop smallpox from terrorizing their family by performing rituals and providing offerings to the evil kami. Rather than putting up red prints of protective deities, some villagers would erect a shrine specifically for Hōsōgami. In these shrines, they prayed and begged for the kami to spare them from his terrible infection.

Some even believed that the kami was not at all the cause of the infection; instead, he was their savior. Those who survived the disease would sometimes give offerings to the kami as a sign of gratitude. Those who did not build a shrine for Hōsōgami would erect one for either Sukunabikona, the Shinto god of healing, or the legendary samurai named Minamoto no Tametomo, who was believed to have once driven a sickness out of the land.

If offerings and prayers did not manage to fend off the evil spirit, the villagers would turn to another ritual called hōsōgami okuri. They would gather around and parade through the streets, beating on drums and bells and creating tunes from their flutes in the hopes they could entertain Hōsōgami and prevent the kami from infecting them.

There are so many stories that revolve around the Shinto gods and spirits, but, of course, some have already been lost in history. While there is said to be a total of twelve Olympians in Greek mythology and about sixty-six gods in the Old Norse belief, Shinto has eight million kami—which is a Japanese phrase describing infinity—and each one of them is to be respected. If one treats a kami with full respect, one will gain many benefits, be it in terms of health, success, wealth, and even examination results. Failure to do so might result in shinbatsu, retribution, which often came in the form of sickness and sometimes even death. When developers decided to cut down a seven-hundred-year-old tree growing in the middle of Kayashima Station back in 1972, many Japanese who strongly believed in Shintoism held a protest. The old tree was said to house a kami, and to let it get cut down by the developers would only bring them terrible misfortune.

Some said that the tree itself began to portray its protest against those who wished it harm. A man was believed to contract hay fever when he tried cutting one of the tree's branches, while some reported seeing a white snake—a type of snake associated with Shinto gods—slithering through the tree branches. Some even spotted smoke coming out of the tree. In the end, none dared to cut down the sacred tree, and it is still standing in the middle of Kayashima Station today.

Purification Rituals

Purification rituals are the central aspect of Shintoism. Indeed, there is no heaven or hell in Shinto, but it is believed that one can never gain blessings from the kami if they remain impure. These impurities can come in many forms. They are called *kegare* and *tsumi*. While *kegare* includes impurities that occur naturally, such as death, disease, menstruation, and filth, *tsumi* focuses more on the violation of legal or religious laws, such as murder, theft, disrespecting a place of worship, and even talking back to your parents. All of these impurities can be cleansed by performing *harae*, a ritual that was first performed by the creator kami, Izanagi.

Purification rituals are also done before taking a step into a Shinto shrine and performing any kind of religious ceremony. The simplest form of purification that can be done before interacting with a kami is called *temizu*. If you ever find yourself in Japan, you should approach the purification fountain called *temizuya* placed at the entrance of a shrine. Use the wooden ladle to draw water from the fountain and then rinse your left hand, followed by your right hand. Pour some water into your hand, and use it to rinse your mouth. Once the purification is done, one is free to enter the shrine and interact with the kami.

Purification can also be done in the form of misogi, which requires a person to cleanse themselves in the ocean or by standing under a cascading waterfall. Shubatsu, on the other hand, is a form of *harae* that uses salt as a purification agent. Shubatsu is often seen at the start of a sumo wrestling match, as the sumo fighters purify the wrestling ring by sprinkling salt around it. Other than water and salt, a ritual wand could also be used to purify not only a person but also objects and land.

Ise Grand Shrine

There are many Shinto shrines scattered throughout the Japanese archipelago. One could find a shrine dedicated to all different kinds of kami, from the kami of rice to money, poetry, and even hair. However, the most sacred Shinto shrine is the one and only Ise Grand Shrine, which is dedicated to none other than the supreme kami of the sun, Amaterasu.

Also known as Ise Jingu, the origins of the shrine go back two thousand years, when Japan was under the reign of Emperor Suinin. According to the *Nihon Shoki*, the emperor requested his daughter, Yamatohime-no-mikoto, set out on a mission in search of a location where they could permanently build a place of worship for the sun goddess. And so, without delaying a single moment, the princess left her dwelling and wandered through the regions of Omi and Mino for over twenty years. She could not find the perfect place for the shrine, so she continued her journey until she suddenly heard the voice of the goddess herself. It was believed that Amaterasu had whispered to the princess of a location where she wished to dwell. This pleasant land chosen by the supreme goddess is known as Ise, and it is located in modern-day Mie Prefecture. Honoring the sun goddess's wish, Yamatohime-no-mikoto placed fifty bells surrounding the area, marking the place for Amaterasu. The princess herself became the first high priestess of the shrine, kicking off the tradition of appointing the emperor's daughter as a high priestess of the Ise Grand Shrine.

Ise Grand Shrine (Naikū).

With the discovery of the land, the inner shrine or Naikū was first built to properly enshrine the sun goddess and house the sacred mirror. This was the same mirror used by the ancient gods to lure Amaterasu out of her cave after the terrible incident with Susanoo. Later on, the same mirror was gifted to the first legendary emperor of Japan, and it remains the imperial regalia of Japan today. About five hundred years after the construction of Naikū, the outer shrine, known as Gekū, was added. It was built six kilometers (about four miles) away from Naikū and is dedicated to Toyouke-Ōmikami, the kami of agriculture and industry who was also said to hold the responsibility of offering sacred food to the sun goddess. While there are over 125 shrines found around Ise, both Naikū and Gekū are what make up the Grand Ise Shrine. However, today, visitors are restricted from entering these two main shrines and are only allowed to roam around the forests and their surrounding areas.

Since the outer and inner shrines are the most sacred sites in Shintoism, they both go through reconstruction once every twenty years. This reconstruction ceremony is known as Shikinen Sengu. It first took place in 690 CE, and the process of rebuilding both shrines takes at least eight years. The entire ceremony also consists of thirty-two rituals, the first one being a ritual that involves cutting the first few trees for the reconstruction of the structures. The last ritual involves the transfer of Amaterasu's sacred mirror into the newly built shrine.

Chapter 5 – The Kofun Period and Early Tomb Building

Queen Himiko was believed to have restored order across the lands of Japan back in the Yayoi period. Before she was chosen by her people to rule, Japan was divided into over a hundred states or tribes, each ruled by a different leader. War was nearly everywhere, as the people were beginning to crave more power and lands for their growing agricultural activities and population. Peace was, no doubt, established when the shaman queen rose to power, as most of the tribes across the islands acknowledged her as a ruler—all except for the Kingdom of Kuna (Kuna-koku)

Little is known about Kuna-koku. The only record that tells its story is about its dispute with the Kingdom of Yamatai. Archaeologists and historians believe that at some point, Himiko sought help from the Chinese to settle the issues going on between the two kingdoms. However, the queen died shortly after. No one has been able to find the reason behind Himiko's death, but we do know that with Himiko gone, peace across the archipelago died as well.

When the queen passed away, another figure rose to power—a king, this time around. But few were fond of the new king, resulting in more bloodshed across Japan. Violent wars erupted yet again, and murder and assassination became the norm. It is believed over a thousand people perished. It seems like with just a snap of a finger, peace was reversed, and the archipelago was in a state of chaos. This continued until people agreed that another woman should be put on the throne. This woman is known in ancient Chinese records as Iyo. She happened to be Himiko's relative; historians believe she was Himiko's niece. At the age of thirteen, Iyo reigned over Japan. She restored order just as Himiko did and maintained a close relationship with China.

In 266 CE, Japan is no longer mentioned in the Chinese records. It was not until the 5th century that Japan would be mentioned again, but by this time, Japan already had its own emperor. No one knows what happened to the Kingdom of Yamatai after Iyo's reign. In fact, even its exact location remains disputed today. If one was to faithfully follow the directions that lead to Yamatai as recorded by the ancient Chinese historians, you would end up south of Japan, right in the middle of the vast Pacific Ocean. Ever since the Edo period, scholars have been trying to trace the location of Yamatai. There are two possible theories today. Himiko's mysterious kingdom could have been located on the west coast of Kyushu or within the central area of Japan, once known as the Yamato region (now known as Nara Prefecture, Honshu).

If the latter theory is taken into account, then it could be possible for researchers to conclude that the Hashihaka Tomb found in the prefecture belonged to none other than the legendary Queen Himiko. And if the massive tomb was, indeed, where the queen was interred, then we could say that Yamatai had some sort of ties with the Yamato, a powerful clan during the Kofun period that gave birth to the imperial house of Japan.

Kofun Tombs and the Birth of a New Period

The Kofun period, which marks its beginning around 250 and lasted until 538 CE, derived its name from the unique burial mounds (also known as kofun) scattered throughout the archipelago. As of today, there are nearly thirty thousand kofun tombs in Japan that have been discovered by archaeologists and scholars. Unlike normal graves and burial mounds, a kofun was initially built only to bury the remains of those who held power and status, such as emperors and powerful clan leaders. Early in this period, the tombs were simpler; they were built on natural mounds and did not have specific designs. However, as time passed, people began building tombs on flat grounds, and more complex designs were introduced, with the most popular one being the keyhole pattern.

These exceptional tombs varied in size, with the smallest measuring about 15 meters (49 miles) in diameter and the biggest measuring at least 821 meters (2,693 miles) long while being encircled by three moats. The latter was also considered the largest kofun with a keyhole design, and it belonged to Japan's sixteenth emperor, Nintoku. Given its massive size, it is not a surprise that the construction took nearly twenty years to complete. Inside of a kofun is normally a stone-lined chamber that often houses a coffin containing the remains of the deceased. Since the ancient Japanese believed in life after death, they would fill the tombs with various precious items, ranging from swords, armors, and shields to bronze mirrors, bracelets, and beads. Haniwa, a type of terracotta clay figure, were also placed around a kofun since they were believed to have the ability to protect the deceased from any kind of danger in the afterlife.

The kofun of Emperor Nintoku.

Although Emperor Nintoku's kofun is believed to be the biggest of all, it was not the oldest one ever found. The Hashihaka kofun located in Nara Prefecture is the oldest keyhole kofun ever discovered, but whose remains were interred there remains a mystery. While some believed that the ancient tomb belonged to the first king of the Yamato Kingdom, the records in the *Nihon Shoki* claim that the tomb belonged to a princess named Yamato-totohi-momoso-hime-no-mikoto.

An aerial view of the Hashihaka kofun.

The princess, who was the daughter of Emperor Kōrei, the seventh legendary emperor of Japan, was also believed to be the wife of Ōmononushi, a Shinto kami of Mount Miwa. The pair, however, never met each other during the day, as the kami refused to appear before his wife in his true form. And so, every night, Ōmononushi would travel to meet with the princess until one day, she demanded him to reveal his true form. Agreeing to the request, Ōmononushi hid in a box—some sources suggest he made his way into the princess's comb case—but the princess was terrified to discover that her husband's true form was a snake. Embarrassed that his wife's reaction upon seeing him was to scream aloud, Ōmononushi slithered his way back into the mountains. The princess was no doubt saddened by the incident. As she took a seat, she accidentally sat on a pair of chopsticks, which stabbed her in her private parts, leading to her death. Her remains were buried in the tomb called Hashihaka, which directly translates to "Chopstick Grave."

There is another theory involving the mystery of this tomb. Some archaeologists claimed that the Hashihaka tomb was actually built for Queen Himiko, who could be the very same person as Princess Yamato-totohi-momoso-hime-no-mikoto. According to Chinese records, a massive tomb was built by the people of Yamatai. It measured at least a hundred paces in diameter, which is almost the same size as the Hashihaka kofun. However, this is but a theory; as of now, no one can conclude whose remains were interred in the tomb. But we can safely say that whoever was buried in the kofun definitely played a role in the rise of the Yamato Kingdom.

The Rise of the Yamato Kingdom

Like the legendary Kingdom of Yamatai, almost every single clan across the Japanese archipelago was led by a religious figure. This includes the Yamato clan. Around the 4th century CE, the Yamato clan rose to power and successfully spread its wings to many other regions in Japan. Legend has it that their success had something to do with a folk hero that went by the name of Yamato Takeru. His entire story was told in the Japanese chronicles of *Kojiki* and *Nihon Shoki*. Yamato Takeru, who was born Prince Ōsu, was one of the sons of the twelfth emperor of Japan, Emperor Keiko.

His story began when he brutally killed his older brother named Ōsu with only his bare hands. Upon discovering the murder, Emperor Keiko decided to punish his son but not with his own hands. Fearing his temper, the emperor sent Yamato Takeru on a mission to conquer the other regions of Japan while secretly hoping that his own son would die while doing so. The prince was sent to the region of Kumaso, where he easily defeated its leaders while they were at a drinking party. With his mission a success, he returned to the emperor, who soon sent him out again on another quest in the eastern region, where he was to eliminate those who opposed the imperial court.

An illustration of Yamato Takeru and the legendary Kusanagi sword.
https://commons.wikimedia.org/wiki/File:Yamato-Takeru-with-Sword-Kusanagi-no-Tsurugi-by-Ogata-Gekko.png

Finally learning that his father had wished nothing but death upon him, Yamato Takeru journeyed to Ise Province and met with the high priestess of Amaterasu, Yamatohime-no-mikoto, who was also his aunt. There, he lamented his father's ill intentions. Feeling sorry for the prince, the high priestess granted him the Kusanagi sword, a sacred weapon obtained by Susanoo, the kami of storms. And so, he continued his quest to the eastern region, where he was suddenly caught in the middle of an ambush. Thanks to the sacred sword, Yamato Takeru successfully countered the attacks, and he managed to conquer many regions in the east. Despite his success, the hero was said to have done atrocious things to the kami of

Mount Ibuki, which led him to be cursed with a mysterious illness that soon led to his death.

While the story of how Yamato Takeru conquered the regions is mostly considered a legend, history tells us that the Yamato clan possibly rose to power due to their blossoming agricultural activities. Intermarriage happened between the Yamato people and powerful figures from other clans throughout the Japanese archipelago. Later on, more and more kofun tombs emerged across the islands. These tombs were considered a symbol of the Yamato; at the time, only those from this clan would be buried in this method. This signifies the growing power of the Yamato clan. The Yamato eventually conquered almost all of Japan, from Kyushu to Tohoku.

During this period, Japan welcomed many immigrants from the Korean Peninsula, who brought new tools and precious knowledge of farming. The Yamato employed these immigrants in their lands and made use of the new farming knowledge they brought with them. With the help of the immigrants, the Yamato Kingdom managed to boost its agricultural economy and wealth. The Yamato rulers realized that they were a step closer to unifying Japan since they had most of the regions under their grasp. However, during this time, Japan was more of a confederation of many other clans. The Yamato ruler was placed on top of this hierarchy, but other clans had their own power and could control their lands how they preferred. Some clans even owned more lands than the imperial family. And so, the Yamato rulers introduced a new bureaucratic ranking system.

In the Yamato court, the head of the Yamato clan took the mantle as an emperor, and only those descended from the clan were able to sit on the Chrysanthemum Throne. As for the other powerful clans or uji, they were granted a kabane, a nobility title. The old clans, such as the Soga and the Katsuragi, were given the kabane title of Omi, which was also a title given to those who had blood relations with the imperial family. Another kabane title,

Muraji, was given to the clans of Otomo, Nakatomi, and Mononobe, which claimed to be descendants of the gods. Then, a single influential figure or leader of these two kabane, Omi and Muraji, would be chosen to carry the title of Ōomi and Ōmuraji, respectively. These two figures acted as direct advisors or ministers to the Yamato court and held a very high position in the government. Aside from these top-tier clans, the mid-level clans were also granted their own kabane, such as Kimi or Atae.

Life in the Kofun Period

While kabane titles were bestowed upon those who held power in a certain clan, the lives of the commoners were not much different compared to the previous period. Most of them still lived in simple dwellings with thatched roofs, except this time around, they replaced their fire pits with a proper earthen stove called a kamado. This kind of oven lasted throughout the centuries and is still used today. The people supported themselves by farming, fishing, and sometimes hunting. Iron became even more common in this period, and it was often used to create farming tools, such as spades, hoes, and sickles.

The people also devoted themselves to nature, a belief they carried over from the Yayoi period. Purification was turned into one of the most important aspects of their beliefs to the point where, every now and then, the Yamato court would send out religious officials to different regions to recite prayers to the communities and rid them of impurities. Other than purification, religious practices during this period included exorcisms and divination rituals, as well as fortune-telling by using burned animal bones.

Punishment systems were further developed, with flogging and banishment being the most common punishments. There were, however, more harsh punishments that existed in this period. When someone committed serious crimes, such as adultery, arson, or murder, the person was almost always sentenced to death. The perpetrator would either be half-buried in the ground before being stoned to death or had their heads sawed off by a piece of bowstring. But how did the community decide who was guilty and who was innocent?

Whenever a dispute between two people could not be resolved privately, they had no other choice but to go through the trial of ordeal or kugatachi. In this trial, the two people accused of being involved in a certain crime were to stand in front of a pot of boiling water and swear their innocence to the gods. Once that was done, they had to put their hands into the boiling water. The one whose hand was wounded the most was considered guilty, as the people believed the gods would protect only the innocent one. The legendary Japanese statesman, Takenouchi no Sukune, was said to have cleared his name from an accusation using this method. The boiling water could also be replaced with a pot containing a poisonous snake. The person who got bitten by the snake would be the one guilty of the crime and must accept their punishment.

Contact with China and Korea

The Kofun period was when Japan started to move toward a more cohesive state. The influences and new knowledge brought by those from the Asian mainland had no doubt helped the people realize their goal, which was to become a more recognized state. By the end of the 4th century, the Yamato state was entangled in a rivalry between three kingdoms in the Korean Peninsula.

The map of the ancient kingdoms of Korea.

These kingdoms were known as Goguryeo (Koguryo), which was the largest among the three; Silla, which dominated the southeastern part of the peninsula; and Baekje in the southwest. On the southern tip of the peninsula was a loose confederation of smaller states known as the Kaya region, which also acted as a doorway for the Yamato to the Korean Peninsula.

The main reason behind the Yamato government's involvement in the war was so they could secure the many sources of iron found in the Korean Peninsula. The Yamato state formed an alliance with the Kingdom of Baekje and went against both Silla and Goguryeo. The Yamato managed to expand their power in some regions in the Korean Peninsula, but they were forced to withdraw by the 6th century CE due to the increasing power of Silla's military forces, which were aided by the Tang dynasty of China.

As for Yamato's contacts with China, the *Book of Song*, a collection of historical records in the Liu Song dynasty, mentioned that five Yamato kings had actively sent them tribute in order to gain recognition and solidify their status as kings or emperors. According to scholars, some of the five Yamato kings could have been the same legendary emperors of Japan named in the *Nihon Shoki*.

By the 5th century CE, the Yamato state once again welcomed another set of migrants from the Asian mainland. These people, also referred to as Toraijin, decided to migrate to the archipelago to escape the raging wars and famine plaguing their homeland. With this migration, the lands of Japan were introduced to new technologies and knowledge, such as irrigation and reservoir construction techniques, shipbuilding, and blacksmithing. Most of the Toraijin were employed by the Yamato court and earned their own kabane titles.

The Kingdom of Baekje also shared a wide variety of knowledge with the Yamato state. Horses were introduced to the archipelago during this period. Through a messenger, the king of Baekje sent a few gifts to the Yamato court. These gifts were literary works called the *Analects of Confucius* and the *Thousand Character Classic*, which is a poem written in Chinese characters. With these two literary works, the Japanese kanji system was born. Japan was finally able to send written diplomatic documents and engraved items to friendly states.

However, the writing system was not the only thing that was introduced by the king of Baekje. A statue of Buddha and Buddhist scriptures were also sent to the court of Yamato, which kickstarted the spread of Buddhism across Japan. This caused a serious quarrel between the state's two main clans.

Chapter 6 – Haniwa and Its Importance

Funeral customs and burial rites have come a long way. Even in this modern world of ours, we can find more than a dozen different ceremonies taking place after the death of a person. If we travel back to ancient times, however, we can discover many funerary practices that might appear normal to those ancient civilizations but perhaps seem strange to our modern minds.

The ancient Egyptians, for instance, had a rather lavish approach to death; they believed that death was not the end and that they would resume their life in the Field of Reeds. Thus, they would often bury the deceased in a tomb filled with goods, ranging from glimmering jewelry to food and weapons. The goods left in these graves acted as supplies for the dead, allowing them to move on to their next life in the celestial field. The ancient Greeks, on the other hand, believed in the underworld or the Land of the Dead. According to legends, the dead must pay a fee to the ferryman named Charon so that they can be transported across the River Styx and reach the underworld. So, when a person died, they would often be buried with an obol, a type of ancient coin that was put inside of the deceased's mouth or over their eyes.

The ancient Japanese also had their own funeral customs. Pit and jar burials were common during the Jomon period, and historians even claim that there were cases where the dead would be buried under a pit house, although the house would then be abandoned. Over time, the ancient Japanese changed the way they honored the dead, especially those who had high status and power. Soon, burial mounds and more complex tombs could be seen scattered throughout the archipelago, especially near the end of the Yayoi period and throughout the Kofun period.

As explained in the previous chapter, the Kofun period earned its name from the distinctive tombs and burial mounds discovered in Japan. While most of these tombs were significantly massive and could span hundreds of meters, another unique feature that made them even more interesting was the terracotta clay figures surrounding the upper section of these tombs. They are known today as Haniwa.

Although archaeologists have discovered many of these clay figures around the tombs, no one is entirely certain of the origins of Haniwa. A writing system did not yet exist during this period, so there was no written record that could tell us the purpose of these clay figures. Some suggest that its origins could be traced back to the Jomon period when the Japanese people created the Dogū, a type of humanoid figure also made out of clay. However, the production of Dogū stopped as soon as the period ended, as archaeologists have not yet found one that dates back to the Yayoi period. The only story that tells us the origin of Haniwa can be seen in the *Nihon Shoki*. The record, however, was written centuries after Haniwa was first introduced, so whether or not the story bears the truth remains unknown.

The Man Possibly Responsible for the Creation of Haniwa

Emperor Suinin, the eleventh legendary emperor of Japan, was said to have contributed several things to Japan. He was the one who instructed his daughter, Yamatohime-no-mikoto, to create a shrine for Amaterasu, leading to the construction of the Ise Grand Shrine. He is also regarded as the one who created sumo wrestling, as the first-ever sumo match was held during his reign.

The story of the first creation of Haniwa began when Emperor Suinin received the news of his half-brother's death. During his reign, it was completely normal for a great number of attendants or servants to follow their lords to the grave. Some suggest that these people were buried alive in the burial mounds, while others claim that they were buried only up to their necks so that they could mourn and wail for the death of their lord. This tradition could even be seen when Queen Himiko died; at least a hundred of her servants were sacrificed for her burial. As for Emperor Suinin, this tradition was carried out when his brother died. Witnessing the many sacrifices, he began to wonder if there was a way to replace the old tradition.

Emperor Suinin was later devastated due to yet another death of a loved one. This time around, it was his wife, Empress Hibasuhime. Once again, the thought of replacing the sacrificial tradition came to mind. The emperor then consulted his ministers and asked for advice regarding the tradition. They suggested sticking with the old ways. Shortly after, the emperor heard another idea from Nomi no Sukune, the legendary sumo wrestler. He suggested that they leave the tradition behind, especially since they were aiming to create a more humane government. He then went on to gather three hundred potters and instructed them to create clay figures.

After being presented with the clay figures, Emperor Suinin agreed to replace the old sacrificial tradition. Instead of sacrificing servants and loyal attendants, the clay figures were used to accompany the dead. To thank Nomi no Sukune for his brilliant idea, the emperor granted him the kabane title of Haji. He would be responsible for overseeing the pottery workers and funeral customs.

How Haniwa Were Made and the Theories of What They Were Used For

Somewhat similar to the previous pottery items found in the Jomon period, the process of making a Haniwa started with a lump of water-based clay. The Japanese used a specific technique called wazumi, which required them to create the image of the Haniwa one layer at a time. The basic shape of the Haniwa, which was normally under a meter tall, was created first. Once it was done, the potters would move on to shape the protruding parts of the figure before they were attached to the main body of the Haniwa created earlier. Other carvings were then added to create more details, and any rough surfaces were smoothed out with a wooden paddle. When they were done with the design, the Haniwa would then be fired at a low temperature.

Since the clay figures had to be fired at a relatively low temperature, it would have taken a long time until you could finally see the end result. So, most emperors and elite members of the ruling family would often plan ahead for their tombs. Haniwa would be prepared way before their deaths so that everything would be ready when death finally came to take these people away from the land of the living.

While the *Nihon Shoki* briefly explained that Haniwa were used to replace an old tradition where slaves were sacrificed and buried with their masters, another theory suggests that these clay figures were actually used to protect the deceased. There is also another theory that claims the opposite; instead of defending the remains of the dead and ensuring the tomb was never disturbed, the Haniwa were actually arranged surrounding a kofun tomb so that they could protect the living from the spirits of the dead. Science, however, suggests that Haniwa were used to avoid corrosion, but which one of these theories is the most accurate remains unknown.

The Evolution of the Haniwa

Aside from providing us with an insight into the evolving art and culture of the Kofun period, the shapes and images of these clay figures also give us a chance to take a glimpse into the early lives of the Japanese people: how they were dressed, what their houses looked like, what their beliefs were. In the early years after the introduction of Haniwa (250–450 CE), they were only made in simple shapes. Many cylindrical Haniwa were discovered by archaeologists, and these are considered to be the earliest forms. As the years passed and bigger kofun tombs started to emerge throughout the archipelago, the Haniwa evolved into more elaborate structures—some even measured more than 1.5 meters (nearly 5 feet) tall.

The Haniwa began to appear in the forms of animals, humans, and even buildings. Clay figures in the shape of a horse were discovered by archaeologists. The horse's tack, collar, saddle, and what seems to be bells resembled those of the Korean Peninsula. Birds, monkeys, wild boars, rabbits, and ships were also common shapes of a Haniwa. Although the outer perimeter of the kofun tombs was often surrounded by cylindrical Haniwa, certain mounds feature house-shaped Haniwa at the center, which could be purposely arranged to resemble a small village or settlement once overseen by the owner of the kofun. These house-shaped Haniwa normally had a thatched roof, a square base complete with simple walls, an entrance, and a couple of rectangular holes as windows.

A Haniwa in the form of a horse.
Gary Todd from Xinzheng, China, CC0, via Wikimedia Commons:
https://commons.wikimedia.org/wiki/File:Haniwa_Terracotta_Figurine_(29768242710).jpg

A house Haniwa.
Gary Todd from Xinzheng, China, CC0, via Wikimedia Commons:
https://commons.wikimedia.org/wiki/File:Haniwa_Terracotta_Figurine_(30028141366).jpg

Perhaps the most famous Haniwa figure is the warrior dressed in early Japanese-style armor called *kikkō*. Excavated from a site in Gunma Prefecture, this Haniwa warrior stands on an elevated cylindrical base and has a height of over 130 centimeters (53 inches) in total. In one of his hands is a sword, while the other could be holding a broken piece of a bow. The wrist guard on his left arm was probably worn to protect himself from the bowstring once he shot an arrow. At the back of the Haniwa was a bow quiver, which further suggests that he was an archer.

Due to this, it is thought that fully armored soldiers had already existed during this period. It could also be a depiction of a soldier from the Mononobe clan, who was entrusted by the emperor to oversee the Yamato Kingdom's military affairs. Some also suggest influence from the Asian mainland; its hip-length armor, gauntlets, and riveted helmet resembled the soldiers of the Chinese horsemen of the Six Dynasties period.

Of course, the designs of Haniwa were not only limited to warriors and soldiers. There were also figures that resembled working farmers, musicians, dancers, and mothers carrying her child in her arms. A female shaman was one of the most intricate forms of Haniwa ever discovered by archaeologists. They would often be seen with a flat headdress and a colored tattoo on their faces. The protruding pendants could symbolize either stone or glass beads, and the flat, circular discs hanging from the Haniwa's belt could represent mirrors, especially since they were considered sacred in Shinto beliefs.

Haniwa of a female shaman.
Daderot, CC0, via Wikimedia Commons:
https://commons.wikimedia.org/wiki/File:Haniwa_in_the_form_of_a_female_shaman,_Jap
an,_Kofun_period,_300-552_AD,_earthenware_-
_Asian_Art_Museum_of_San_Francisco_-_DSC01442.JPG

Haniwa in the Modern World

The number of kofun tombs might have declined as the years passed, and so did the existence of Haniwa. Indeed, it took many years for Haniwa to be rediscovered by modern archaeologists, but its unique design and mysteries did not only invite us to take a look at the early lives of the ancient Japanese but also opened the door for modern artists to appreciate the arts of the ancient Japanese people. Many began to show interest and saw the aesthetic significance in Haniwa. Isamu Noguchi, a renowned American artist in the mid-20th century, fell in love with the beauty of Haniwa when he first saw one during his visit to Kyoto Museum in 1931. From then onward, the American artist began to study more about the clay figure to the point where he had created several masterpieces heavily inspired by Haniwa. *Time* even named Haniwa a form of "pure art."

By the end of the 20th century, Haniwa began to receive even more attention from the world. It is safe to say that Haniwa are now forever immortalized, as they have been featured in an array of entertainment mediums, ranging from films, tv shows, video games, and even trading cards, though they are often depicted in a less complex form compared to the ones discovered from excavation sites and displayed behind glass in a museum.

Chapter 7 – Life in the Asuka Period

Assassinations, murders, conflicts, great changes, and the spread of Buddhism—these are the words that might come to mind whenever the Asuka period is mentioned. The Asuka period only lasted nearly two centuries (538-710 CE), but one cannot deny that it brought many changes to Japan, allowing it to become the flourishing country that we know today. Although the period started off rough, with clans constantly at each other's throats, spilling blood for the sake of power, the Japanese archipelago soon witnessed a gradual improvement in both political and social organizations as time passed. Buddhism was introduced to the Japanese people, greater ties were made with China, new ruling systems were established to minimize corruption in the Yamato government, and new art, architecture, and other facets of culture surfaced.

The Conflict between the Soga and Mononobe Clans

The origins of the Soga remain uncertain. They claimed to be descendants from a powerful clan named Katsuragi, while some scholars believe they were initially a family from the Korean Peninsula that eventually made the Asuka region their base. They then went on to form alliances with the Toraijin clans and made use of their knowledge to establish themselves as one of the greatest clans in the Yamato state. The Soga clan rose to greater heights of power during the reign of Emperor Kinmei. Soga no Iname, the clan's leader, who also held the title of Ōomi, was said to have strengthened his clan's power and ties to the imperial family by marrying his two daughters to Emperor Kinmei. To Soga no Iname's delight, his two daughters eventually bore children with the emperor; three of them sat on the Chrysanthemum Throne. Through marital relationships, Soga no Iname successfully increased the Soga clan's status and influence throughout Japan.

The Mononobe clan, on the other hand, claimed to be descendants of the gods, and like the Nakatomi, they held strong Shinto beliefs. Since this was another influential clan in the Yamato state, the position of Ōmuraji was often filled by the leaders of the Mononobe clan, which means they were put in charge of military matters.

When a statue of Buddha arrived in the archipelago in 538 CE, the ruling emperor at that time, Emperor Kinmei, was torn between spreading the new religion to his people or rejecting it completely and sticking to Shintoism. So, he consulted his two high ministers, the Ōomi, Soga no Iname, and the Ōmuraji, Mononobe no Okoshi. Soga no Iname had close contact with people from the Asian mainland, and he right away agreed to accept the new religion. Mononobe no Okoshi strongly disagreed, as he claimed that adopting Buddhism would anger the Shinto gods. After listening to both of his ministers' explanations, the emperor decided to entrust the Buddha statue to Soga no Iname for the time being. Soga no Iname soon built a brand-new Buddhist temple. The Ōomi kept the Buddha statue in the temple and began to adopt the new religion. At the same time, a terrible plague took over the lands, killing many of the inhabitants.

Mononobe no Okoshi saw the plague as a misfortune brought by the Shinto gods as a result of blindly accepting the new religion. He voiced this belief to Emperor Kinmei, who later gave him permission to resolve the matter. Without delay, Mononobe no Okoshi burned down the Buddhist temple built by his rival and cast the Buddha statue into the river, thus starting a war between the Soga and Mononobe clans.

Many years passed by, and the conflict between the two clans had only gotten worse. After the death of Soga no Iname, his son, who went by the name Soga no Umako, continued his legacy. Meanwhile, the title of Ōmuraji passed to Mononobe no Moriya. When Emperor Yōmei (the son of Emperor Kinmei and the thirty-first emperor of Japan) died, another dispute erupted between the two powerful clans. Soga no Umako was planning to place his nephew on the throne, while Mononobe no Moriya decided to enthrone another candidate, Prince Anahobe. However, the dispute came to an end when Soga no Umako assassinated Prince Anahobe, which allowed his nephew, Sushun, to ascend to the Chrysanthemum Throne.

The feud between the two clans did not stop there. Soga no Umako decided to end the conflict once and for all, and he rallied his allies in the imperial court and attacked the Mononobe residence. War was waged with Mononobe no Moriya, who led his troops while firing arrows from on top of a tree. The Soga were forced to retreat more than once; the Mononobe clan was quite powerful when it came to their military. However, legend has it that the tides were about to turn when the fourteen-year-old Prince Shōtoku, a devout Buddhist, began to pray for Soga's victory. Perhaps Prince Shōtoku's prayer was heard, as shortly after, an arrow struck Mononobe no Moriya, which led to his death. With their leader gone, the Soga clan managed to destroy the entire Mononobe family. The victory of the Soga marked the beginning of the spread of Buddhism across Japan.

The fall of the Mononobe clan also meant the abolishment of the Ōmuraji title. Soga no Umako no doubt held the highest power in the imperial court, and his growing influence somehow worried Emperor Sushun. One day, a wild boar was presented before the emperor, and as he held a *kōgai* (a type of Japanese hairdressing tool) to stab the boar's eye, he muttered something that drew Soga no Umako's attention. The emperor said that one day, he would kill a man that he hated just as he killed the poor boar. Soga no Umako quickly came to the conclusion that he was the person the emperor was speaking of and that, sooner or later, he would be deposed and replaced by someone else. So, the Ōomi planned another assassination. The emperor was killed by a man named Yamato no Aya no Koma. With a vacancy on the throne, Soga no Umako put his niece, who was also the younger sister of Emperor Yōmei, on the throne. The empress was known by the name Suiko.

Empress Suiko

Toyomike Kashikiya hime no Mikoto, more famously known as Empress Suiko, was the thirty-third ruler of Japan and the first woman to ascend to the Chrysanthemum Throne. The empress ruled after the murder of her half-brother, Emperor Sushun, in 592 until she passed away in 628. Like those from the Soga clan, Empress Suiko was also pro-Buddhist. Some even claimed she had taken the vows of a Buddhist nun before accepting the throne. She highly encouraged the influence of Chinese culture across the archipelago.

The following year after her ascension to the throne, a regent was appointed to assist her; this position was given to none other than Prince Shōtoku. Empress Suiko and her regent are often credited with the spread of Buddhism in Japan. In just the span of two years, the empress issued the Flourishing Three Treasures Edict, which established Buddhism as Japan's national religion. From there, the religion thrived throughout every part of the archipelago, and new temples were constructed. More Buddhist monks and scholars were employed by the government, with most of them carrying influences from China. These foreign cultures then blended with the Japanese traditional cultures, resulting in the Asuka culture.

The empress, however, did not shun those who still held strong beliefs in Shintoism. In fact, Buddhism and Shintoism coexisted peacefully during her reign. It was said that when a devastating earthquake struck Yamato Province back in 599, the empress ordered several constructions of Shinto shrines in honor of the earthquake kami.

Although many viewed her as merely a puppet under the influence of Soga no Umako, the empress was actually a strong political leader. Soga no Umako once requested Kazuraki no Agata, an imperial territory, to be granted to him, but the empress had no issues rejecting the Ōomi's request. This shows that the empress was not entirely powerless.

Asuka Culture, Art, and Architecture

Foreign influences, especially those from China and Korea, played a prominent role in developing the unique Asuka culture. At that time, Japan employed many Korean architects to construct new structures and even gardens. Empress Suiko once commissioned a Korean craftsman to build the very first palace garden in Japan. Heavily influenced by China, the garden featured a pond and an artificial mountain that represented Mount Mera, a sacred five-peaked mountain in Buddhist cosmology. Buddhist structures and statues were also common in Japan by this period, with most of them being created out of wood and gilded bronze.

Japan absorbed influences from other parts of the globe, such as ancient Greece and India. This can be seen in Hōryū-ji Temple, which was built by Prince Shōtoku in 607. It featured pillars similar to those found in ancient Greece's Parthenon. The Tori style, named after Japan's first and greatest sculptor, Kuratsukuri Tori, also emerged during the Asuka period. Influenced by sculptures from the Northern Wei, Tori's best masterpiece was the Shaka

Triad, which was built in 623 and served as a memorial for Prince Shōtoku.

Hōryū-ji in Nara Prefecture, Japan.

The Asuka period also introduced many unique paintings that were influenced by Buddhism. One example was Tamamushi-no Zushi, also known as the Jewel-Beetle Shrine. Resembling a miniature shrine, Tamamushi-no-Zushi housed a Buddha sculpture, where people often placed a range of offerings in front of it, such as rice, vegetables, tea, and flowers. Unfortunately, we can no longer take a glimpse of the old Buddha statue since it has been lost; some said that it was stolen in the 10th century.

However, the most prominent feature of the shrine can still be found today. On the lower part of the shrine were several panels containing paintings that depicted scenes from the previous lives of Buddha. One of the most popular ones is a painting of Prince Mahasattva jumping off a cliff to save a tigress and her cubs from starvation.

A panel on the lower left of Tamamushi-no Zushi depicting Prince Mahasattva sacrificing himself to save a starving tigress.
https://commons.wikimedia.org/wiki/File:Tamamushi_Shrine_(lower_left).jpg

With the existence of a writing system, which was introduced during the late Kofun period, the Japanese, especially the nobles and elites, were now able to read, write, and keep written records of history and literature. This no doubt led to a more developed nation. The art of poems also began to see its beginnings during this period, which was later compiled in the *Manyoshu* circa 760.

The Twelve Cap Ranks

Before the establishment of the Twelve Cap Ranks in the imperial court, the title of kabane was mostly hereditary. If one was born into a mid-level clan, it was nearly impossible to obtain a higher rank, no matter one's achievements and success. The Twelve Cap Ranks system was created to rectify this. Instead of earning titles based on family lines, this system allowed a person to be promoted based on their merit and individual achievements.

The written Japanese records did not exactly mention who established the system, but many historians believe that, under the blessings of the empress, Prince Shōtoku and Soga no Umako were the ones who reinforced this new system after witnessing it being used by the Sui dynasty of China and the kingdoms of Korea, Baekje and Goguryeo. Under this system, officials were required to wear silk caps of different colors that signified their ranks. Some say that it was the color of the feather on their caps that differentiated them, not the cap itself. Nevertheless, each of the ranks was named after six Confucian virtues, and each of them was divided into two lower ranks.

The Seventeen Article Constitution

In 604, a year after the introduction of the Twelve Cap Ranks, came the Seventeen Article Constitution. Drafted by Prince Shōtoku, who infused the influences of Confucian principles and the understandings of Buddhism, the constitution's sole purpose was to ensure a smoothly running government. Japan was moving toward a unified state, one that was ruled by a single sovereign. Through this constitution, the emperor's position was strengthened, as they were regarded as the highest authority in the hierarchy.

Since the emperor or empress was placed on top, their subjects were to respect and obey their decisions and actions at all times. The imperial court's officials were to be employed based on their merits instead of heredity. The constitution also highlighted the responsibilities of the ruler and their officials.

Envoys to the Sui Dynasty

A century after Japan's last envoy to China, which had been deployed by the five kings of Wa, Prince Shōtoku (during the reign of Empress Suiko) was believed to have sent the first embassy to the Sui dynasty in 600. This event, however, was not recorded in the *Nihon Shoki*, but it was mentioned in the Chinese record called the *Book of Sui.*

During the embassy's visit, Emperor Wen asked the Japanese messenger about the nation's customs and government. After receiving an answer, the emperor was said to have had a different opinion of the way Japan was governed at that time. He thought the ruling system lacked justice and was completely irrational. Emperor Wen then urged the messenger to return to his land and have his king rectify his customs. This unfortunate embassy was probably the reason the visit was not included in the Japanese records. It could also be plausible that Prince Shōtoku decided to devise his two main reforms—the Twelve Cap Ranks and the Seventeen Article Constitution—in response to Emperor Wen's comments.

Another envoy was again sent to the Sui dynasty seven years later, and it was led by Ono no Imoko. When Ono no Imoko arrived in China, he presented a letter to Emperor Yang, the ruling emperor of the Sui dynasty at that time. The said letter began with the sentence: "The emperor of the land of the rising sun sends this letter to the emperor of the land where the sun sets."

This particular sentence irritated Emperor Yang due to the Japanese ruler using the word "emperor," which somehow indicated that they were on the same level. So, the Chinese emperor told his ministers of his wish to never set eyes on such a horrible letter ever again. But despite the emperor's response, the diplomatic relationship between China and Japan did not end there, as the Sui dynasty sent an embassy in return to Japan. This embassy was led by Hai Seisei. Although Emperor Yang did not give any direct response, the embassy sent to Japan showed that the Sui dynasty somehow recognized the ruler of Japan as an independent sovereign.

It is also believed that Emperor Yang sent a letter to the Japanese ruler through Ono no Imoko, but the diplomat claimed that the letter was lost at sea. Scholars suggest that he intentionally destroyed the letter, knowing that the unpleasant contents would enrage the empress. His action resulted in exile. However, Ono no Imoko was given amnesty soon after, and he had the honor of being promoted to the first grade of the Twelve Cap Ranks for his excellent service.

The following year, another embassy led by Ono no Imoko was sent to the Sui dynasty to accompany Hai Seisei back to his homeland. This time around, Ono no Imoko brought along several scholars and monks who extended their stay in China to gather new knowledge and skills. All of the knowledge obtained by the scholars were used to benefit Japan and kickstarted the many unique customs in Japan that we see today.

The Overbearing Power of the Soga Clan That Led to Their Destruction

After accomplishing many achievements in his life as a regent, Prince Shōtoku was finally laid to rest in 622. With the legendary prince gone, the power in the imperial court was almost entirely monopolized by the Soga clan. The clan was now led by Soga no Emishi, the son of Soga no Umako.

Soga no Emishi first displayed his disobedience and craving for power when he appointed his own son, Soga no Iruka, into the imperial court without consulting the empress and other high officials. The father and son then proceeded to construct residences high up on a hill, overlooking the imperial palace. This irritated many since it signified that they were above the imperial family. Soga no Iruka even went to the extent of referring to his sons as princes.

To make matters worse, Soga no Iruka laid an attack on the residence of Prince Shōtoku's son, Prince Yamashiro. The incident went horribly. Prince Yamashiro and his family were forced to commit suicide, thus ending the great Prince Shōtoku's direct bloodline.

These changes in the state were eyed by Nakatomi no Kamatari, an important statesman and aristocrat. After witnessing the growing power of the Soga clan and knowing that it could possibly lead

Japan to its doom, Nakatomi decided to put an end to the clan's greedy monopoly once and for all. And so, he began plotting a strategy to overthrow the Soga clan by conspiring with the imperial prince, Naka no Ōe.

On July 10th, 645, Soga no Iruka attended a court ceremony in Daigokuden (the Great Hall of State), where he welcomed the diplomats arriving from the Korean kingdoms. Prince Naka no Ōe had hidden a spear in the hall. He bribed several palace guards and was waiting for an opportunity to get rid of Soga no Iruka. He had initially ordered four men to ambush Iruka, but it became clear that they had cold feet. The prince did not want to waste the opportunity, so he grabbed the hidden spear and severely wounded Iruka. The latter, however, did not die on the spot. He claimed to be innocent and begged Empress Kōgyoku (the ruling empress at this time) to hold an investigation. The empress agreed, and as she left the hall, the four armed men suddenly emerged and immediately killed Soga no Iruka.

The news of his son's death reached Soga no Emishi shortly after. He could not contain his despair, so he burned his entire residence and committed suicide. With that, the Soga clan was permanently erased, and the Japanese government was finally free of its power. However, this bloody incident (known in history as the Isshi Incident) was not the only thing planned by Prince Naka no Ōe and Nakatomi no Kamatari. Having successfully removed the Soga clan, the two men then moved on to the next step: reconstructing the Yamato government and transitioning into a new era.

Chapter 8 – The Spread of Buddhism

When speaking of Buddhism and its religious practices, many would immediately think of meditation, karma, reincarnation, and perhaps massive Buddha statues, which were built for Buddhism's many temples around the world. But truth be told, Buddhism is way more than just that. In fact, this two-and-a-half millennia religion consists of many complex yet amazing religious practices, beliefs, and principles that changed the course of many nations, including Japan. The origins of Buddhism can be traced back to the 5th century BCE, which makes it one of the oldest religions in the world. Today, Buddhism is practiced by over five hundred million people around the globe, with its influence most prominent in both East and Southeast Asia.

The Origin of Buddhism and How It Was Spread to the World

Buddhism began with a man who went by the name Siddhartha Gautama. He was initially a son of King Suddhodana and Queen Maya, the rulers of the ancient city named Kapilavastu. After his birth (circa 563 BCE), the king and queen were said to have been approached by an old hermit named Asita, who also served the king as his advisor. The hermit informed the royal pair of a prophecy, saying that their son bore a magnificent destiny. He would grow up to either become a powerful king or a spiritual leader if he ever saw the lives of those outside the palace compound.

As soon as King Suddhodana heard the prophecy, he decided to protect his son from seeing the sufferings of the world to prevent the prophecy from coming true. So, the prince remained within the palace for twenty-nine years of his life without having a single glimpse of life outside the palace gates. Not once did he ever witness suffering or any unpleasant experience. Some say that the king even went to the extent of sweeping away the fallen petals of a wilting flower and sending his sick and old servants away. Because of this, the prince was completely unaware of the process of aging, death, and even sickness.

However, it all changed one day when the prince listened to a musician sing about the wonders of the world. Enthralled by what could be on the other side of the palace walls, Siddhartha Gautama went to see the king and informed him of his wish to travel and see the world. Although the king was hesitant at first, he finally granted his son's wish. King Suddhodana told his son that in order to prepare himself to be the future king, he must see the world that he would soon be ruling.

During his travels, Siddhartha Gautama encountered the first of the Four Signs—a man who was coughing continuously. Since the prince had never witnessed any type of sickness before, he asked his royal charioteer about the man's condition. He was told that the man was battling a sickness and that it was completely normal since everyone would get sick at some point in their lives. The prince was, of course, surprised by this revelation, but he continued his journey across the kingdom.

Shortly after, he encountered the second and third of the Four Signs: an old man and a person who had just died. Again, the prince turned to his charioteer, who explained that these events were inevitable. Again, this revelation saddened Siddhartha Gautama, and he finally came to the realization that he, too, would experience the events he had just witnessed, as would the ones he loved most. Continuing on his adventure, Siddhartha Gautama encountered the fourth and last of the Four Signs: a wanderer who was sitting still. The wanderer had explained to the prince that he was meditating and that he had left all his material things behind to embark on a spiritual journey to discover an escape from life's suffering.

Inspired by the wanderer, Siddhartha Gautama began his own quest to search for ways to end suffering. After renouncing his wealth and nobility, he traveled far from his kingdom, trying to gain more and more knowledge until he finally decided to join five ascetics who were meditating deep in the woods. There, Siddhartha Gautama devoted himself to extreme deprivation, believing that he could finally achieve enlightenment this way. He fasted for six years and only survived by consuming a few grains of rice each day. However, Gautama soon realized that this deprivation was making his state worse than before. His ribs were visible due to long-term starvation, and his mind had slowed down. So, he left the ascetics and encountered a woman who offered him rice and milk. After restoring his energy, Siddhartha Gautama came to the conclusion that neither indulgence nor extreme deprivation could provide a path to enlightenment. It had to lay between those two extremes. This idea was later developed into the Middle Path.

Continuing his journey, Siddhartha Gautama came across a fig tree (now known as the Bodhi Tree), and he sat underneath it. After meditating for forty-nine consecutive days under the tree, Siddhartha Gautama finally attained enlightenment. At the age of thirty-five, Gautama became the "Awakened One," although he is more famously known as the Buddha.

The Buddha then returned to the five ascetics in the woods and shared his knowledge. This was when he delivered the first dharma and shared the Four Noble Truths. With his teachings, the ascetics soon became the first members of the Sangha (the Buddhist community), and Buddha went on to spread his teachings across the Gangetic Plain, doing so until he passed away at the age of eighty. Despite his death, Buddhism still spread throughout the world. Buddha's teachings were recorded in texts known as the sutras, which were later spread around the globe. They traveled from the Ganges region to Sri Lanka and other regions in Southeast Asia before moving on to both Central and East Asia. From there, Buddhism made its way to Mongolia, Russia, and finally to the countries in the west.

Buddhism in Japan

Japan saw the arrival of Buddhism through a diplomatic relationship with the Korean Peninsula. Ironically, when Buddhism, a religion often associated with peace and enlightenment, first emerged in the Japanese archipelago, it somehow caused a feud between two of the most important clans of the Yamato Kingdom. This was because Buddhism was not only used as a religion but also in political matters. Soga no Umako, for example, wished to spread the religion not only because of its teachings but also because he saw it as an opportunity to bolster his authority. Wars were waged, and blood was spilled. After the issue was resolved, the religion was spread to every corner of the islands, allowing Japan to embrace a more civilized and organized way of life.

Japan already had its own governing system before the arrival of Buddhism. The Yamato clan was the first to rise to power and claim the throne of Japan. They called themselves kings and queens—the term emperor was not officially used until the reign of Emperor Tenmu—but their power was often overshadowed by the powerful clan chieftains. However, with the arrival of Buddhism, the nation started to make some great changes, focusing more on solidifying the emperor's power and moving toward a centralized government.

Buddhism was then made the nation's official religion almost immediately after Empress Suiko first sat on the Chrysanthemum Throne. A proper constitution was compiled by Prince Shōtoku; it heavily relied on the combination of Buddhist beliefs and Confucian principles. Emperors and empresses were put at the top of the hierarchy, and they were to be obeyed and respected at all times. New ranking systems were introduced to appoint and promote officials. Moral codes were emphasized, and due to a more organized and stable political system, contacts were made with China. Monks were often sent there to learn and bring back knowledge in various fields.

Aside from the nation's governing system, Buddhism also greatly affected culture, art, and architecture. The level of literacy skyrocketed with the arrival of Buddhism, which had been introduced by Baekje. Japan finally had a writing system, and historical records could be compiled. The Japanese people, especially the elites and nobles, could now read and write. Paintings and sculptures became more intricate and complex, and they were heavily influenced by the new religion. Bronze statues of Buddha became a normal sight, along with paintings that depicted the previous lives of bodhisattvas (beings who delay their enlightenment to assist others). However, the most obvious change after the arrival of Buddhism could be seen in the construction of many temples across the Japanese islands.

After scoring a victory against the Mononobe clan and contributing to the establishment of Buddhism in Japan, Soga no Umako built Hōkō-ji (now known as Asuka-dera), one of the first and oldest fully-fledged Buddhist temples in Japan. Prince Shōtoku also honored his promise and erected a temple named Shitennō-ji in modern-day Osaka. By the 6th century CE, the archipelago housed a huge number of Buddhist temples and monasteries. The number continued to grow after the end of the Asuka period. Emperor Shōmu, who ruled during the Nara period, for instance, suggested the construction of provincial temples across the Japanese archipelago. He believed that Buddhism could put a stop to the political turmoil that was happening during his reign.

These temples were a sign of power. Before the arrival of Buddhism, kofun tombs were built for powerful chieftains, emperors, empresses, and the royal family. The size of these tombs signified their power and status, but as Buddhism spread, the construction of these massive tombs greatly decreased. Instead, temples were built, and they soon replaced the tombs. Bigger and greater temples meant powerful and influential emperors.

Buddhism vs. Shintoism

Although both Buddhism and Shintoism are closely knit together, there are still several differences that remind us that they are, indeed, two separate religions. True, Shintoism originated from Japan itself while Buddhism originated in India, but the biggest difference that completely distinguishes the two religions is their purpose.

Shintoism is the way of life. Its devotees hold their beliefs in the kami. They believe that by respecting the kami, their lives will be blessed. People are believed to be born as pure as the driven snow. The only thing that could stop them from receiving blessings is impurities. To put this in simple words, the purpose of Shintoism is for its devotees to lead an honest life and respect the kami. In return, their lives are blessed.

However, in Buddhism, the purpose is to reach enlightenment. Buddhists believe that life itself is a cycle of suffering. So, those who practice Buddhism strive to achieve a state of enlightenment so that they do not have to experience another cycle of suffering.

Other differences can be seen in the deities that are worshiped. Buddhism does not have any deities, although there are supernatural beings that can help guide someone to enlightenment. On the other hand, Shintoism has an unlimited number of kami since they believe that a spirit dwells in all of our surroundings. Buddhism also has clear doctrines and rules, while Shintoism has neither specific texts nor teachings and doctrines.

The two religions have interesting differences in the description of their lands of the dead or the underworld. Shinto's underworld is called Yomi, but unlike hell, it is not a place where the deceased face their mistakes and get punished. It is also not heaven; rather, it is merely a place where the dead carry on.

Buddhism has its own version of the underworld, and it is known as Jigoku. Buddhists believe in reincarnation, and they also believe that the state of their rebirth is intertwined with karma. If a person lived a life filled with good actions and deeds, they would be reborn in one of the heavenly realms. Bad karma, however, can lead a person to be reborn in Jigoku, although they won't remain there permanently. According to the scrolls made in the Heian period, Jigoku consisted of several different hells, each reserved for different types of crimes and wrongdoings. Murdering another human being or even an animal will cause the person to end up in Toukatsu Jigoku or the Reviving Hell, where they would be beaten to death repeatedly by an oni (a demon-like figure). The punishment will only stop when the karma of the misdeeds is all used up. Only then would the person be reborn into a better realm.

How Buddhism and Shinto Coexist

Shintoism was never erased from the lands of Japan with the arrival of Buddhism. In modern Japan, one can easily see a Shinto shrine placed side by side with Buddhist temples. Some Japanese people might identify themselves as Buddhist while still practicing Shinto rituals and attending Shinto-related ceremonies. Many even have Shinto shelves and Buddhist altars in their home. Wedding ceremonies often include Shinto rituals, while funeral rites tend to be entrusted to Buddhism. This proves that Buddhism and Shinto coexist peacefully.

But when exactly did the lines between these two religions blur? The amalgamation of these two religions is called Shinbutsu-shūgō, and it began during the Nara period when a *jingū-ji* or a shrine temple was first built. Before the people erected Daibutsu (Giant

Buddha) in Tōdai-ji Temple, a Buddhist priest was said to have visited the Ise Grand Shrine to inform the kami Amaterasu of the construction. To help protect the temple, the priest installed a shrine of Hachiman, the Shinto kami of war and culture, in the compound of Tōdai-ji. Ever since this event, Shinto shrines have been constructed near Buddhist temples.

A depiction of Hachiman in Buddhist monk attire.
https://commons.wikimedia.org/wiki/File:S%C5%8Dgy%C5%8D_Hachiman.jpg

Later on, priests and monks began to link Shinto kami to Buddhas, as they believed that kami were actually reincarnations of the Buddha. They even suggested that the kami were suffering from the cycle of birth and that they needed to achieve enlightenment. From then on, monks would often read sutras to the kami to assist them in attaining enlightenment. The Shinto god Hachiman was absorbed into Buddhism, where he was also known as Hachiman Daibosatsu. In Buddhism, Hachiman was described as a kami who had become a bodhisattva, a being who had already attained enlightenment but delayed it so they could assist others. While he is often pictured wearing the official garments of an emperor or in full samurai armor while riding a horse, a depiction of Hachiman in Buddhist monk attire also exists.

Buddhism and Shintoism were separated again by order of the government during the Meiji period, as these rulers sought to minimize the spread of Buddhism. Many of the *jingū-ji* were destroyed during this time. However, many years later, the two religions began to coexist again, and it remains this way today.

Chapter 9 – Prince Shōtoku (574– 622)

Japan is renowned for its many legendary figures, both historical and mythical. Emperor Jimmu, for instance, is known as the first emperor of Japan mentioned in the *Nihon Shoki* and *Kojiki*. He was said to be a descendant of Amaterasu through her grandson Ninigi and had ascended to the throne as early as 660 BCE. However, due to the lack of archaeological evidence, historians and scholars alike agree that Jimmu and the eight other emperors who reigned after him did not exist and were merely myths. The same, however, cannot be said about Prince Shōtoku, another famous figure in Japanese history, although there are a few who question whether or not he was a real person.

Sometimes referred to as the founder of the Japanese nation and known as the father of Japanese Buddhism, Prince Shōtoku was, no doubt, the most well-known figure in Japan. Due to his efforts, Buddhism flourished throughout the Japanese archipelago, and his drive to establish a harmonious nation led to the introduction of the Twelve Cap Ranks and the Seventeen Article Constitution. These two political reforms set the foundation for Japan to move into a much more developed and organized nation. Prince Shōtoku's continuous efforts also led to Japan strengthening its relationship with China.

The Early Life of Prince Shōtoku

Prince Shōtoku was the son of Japan's thirty-first emperor, Emperor Yōmei, and his consort, who also happened to be his younger half-sister, Princess Anahobe no Hashihito. Born in the year 574, the prince, according to the *Nihon Shoki*, was said to possess a variety of wonders. The prince was originally named Umayado no ōji; the name means the prince of the stable door (the prince was born in front of a stable). Legend has it that the prince had the ability to speak the moment he entered the world. It was also said that he performed a Buddhist prayer as soon as he turned two years old. The miracles did not stop there, as the ancient semi-mythical record even claims that Prince Shōtoku could listen to ten men speaking simultaneously. Not only was he able to comprehend each of the men's speeches, but he could also easily provide solutions that were rarely wrong.

But, of course, historians agree that these are but myths written to exaggerate the prince's early life. Rather than being born with exceptional gifts—some even claimed he was the reincarnation of Buddha—Prince Shōtoku was said to have been raised within the palace, spending most of his days gaining knowledge from a Korean monk. As he grew up, Prince Shōtoku became well-versed in Buddhist doctrine. Like the elites and nobles, the prince could read and write.

By the age of fourteen, Prince Shōtoku was already involved in the chaotic struggle between the two powerful Soga and Mononobe clans. The Soga clan, which was pro-Buddhist, was adamant about spreading Buddhism across Japan, while the Mononobe wished to remain true to Shinto beliefs. This disagreement resulted in terrible bloodshed, in which the Mononobe had the upper hand due to their experiences in military affairs. Upon witnessing the Soga clan retreat from the war multiple times, Prince Shōtoku, who was already a devout Buddhist at the time, decided to turn to the Shitenno (Four Heavenly Guardians of Buddhism) for help.

The young prince was said to have sat on the ground and spent hours carving statues of the Buddhist deities. Once Prince Shōtoku was done, he prayed to them for the Soga clan's victory. In exchange for their help, he promised to build a temple dedicated to the Four Heavenly Guardians as soon as the war was over. Miraculously, shortly after the prayer, a warrior from the Soga clan shot an arrow that hit the clan leader of the Mononobe right in the chest, which immediately marked the fall of the entire Mononobe clan. With this victory, Japan saw the birth of Buddhism, with Prince Shōtoku soon at the helm.

After the assassination of Emperor Sushun, Soga no Umako's own nephew, the throne was passed to Empress Suiko. She was said to have reigned over Japan for thirty-five years and oversaw great developments. But some believed that the empress could not have achieved her success without the help of Prince Shōtoku. A year after she was chosen as the empress, Prince Shōtoku was appointed as a regent, thus beginning the story of his many accomplishments that made him a famous historical figure.

Prince Shōtoku's Accomplishments and Contributions

When Prince Shōtoku rose to power, he was often pictured wearing Chinese-style court clothes, complete with official headgear and a pair of aristocratic shoes. It was also said that he carried a jeweled sword, which was an imperial symbol of power and authority. At times, the prince would be depicted in ceremonial attire, especially when he was lecturing on the Buddhist sacred texts.

As a regent, the prince went to extra lengths to ensure that his wish to turn Japan into a harmonious state came true. In 600, the ancient Chinese records state that Prince Shōtoku sent an envoy to China, where one of his messengers was asked by the Chinese emperor about Japan's customs. Upon discovering how the Japanese government ruled their lands at that time, the emperor immediately expressed his negative opinion. Some believed that Prince Shōtoku began to work on two of his biggest political reforms in response to the Chinese emperor's critics. And so, three years after the diplomatic envoy returned to the land of the rising sun, Prince Shōtoku introduced Japan to the Twelve Cap Ranks, as well as the first-ever Japanese constitution, the Seventeen Article Constitution, the following year.

Through the Twelve Cap Ranks, Prince Shōtoku made it possible for anyone to get promoted into higher positions in the imperial court, no matter their family lineage. By drafting the Seventeen Article Constitution, the prince managed to solidify the status of the emperor or empress and promote Buddhism as the state's official religion. Ever since he was young, Prince Shōtoku had been heavily influenced by both Buddhist teachings and Confucian principles. He put a lot of emphasis on the importance of harmony, so it is not a surprise that the constitution highlighted moral codes and social behavior. During his lifetime, the corruption rate was said to have decreased compared to the previous periods. No one was allowed to impose taxes on the people unless it was the emperor or empress. Indeed, not every single point in the constitution was practiced during the Asuka period, but it surely played a role in shaping the government in the later periods.

Prince Shōtoku also sent many monks and scholars abroad to gather useful knowledge and skills. He introduced the Chinese-style calendar to Japan and encouraged ties with China. Throughout his time as a regent, Prince Shōtoku sent at least five diplomatic missions to China. He invited scholars from the Asian mainland to Japan so that they could spread knowledge in astronomy, medicine, and geography. The prince himself turned into a scholar, as he has been credited with authoring the commentaries on the three

Mahayana Buddhist scriptures: the Lotus Sutra, the Vimalakirti Nirdesa, and Queen Srimala Sutra.

As you might expect, Prince Shōtoku was a busy man. Staying true to his promise when he first carved the wooden statues of the Shitenno, Prince Shōtoku immediately started the construction of the Shitennō-ji Temple with the help of a few skilled carpenters from the Kingdom of Baekje. The temple, now named one of the oldest temples in Japan, still stands today, although it has gone through multiple restoration projects. With the completion of the Shitennō-ji Temple in 593, the prince then moved on to yet another project. He commissioned another Buddhist temple in Nara Prefecture, which we know as Hōryū-ji Temple. However, an account in the *Nihon Shoki* suggests that lightning once struck the temple, destroying it. But thanks to a reconstruction project done over a thousand years ago, we can still see it today.

The main hall and pagoda of Shitennō-ji.
https://commons.wikimedia.org/wiki/File:Shitenn%C5%8D-ji_main_hall_and_pagoda.png

Another important temple built by the regent prince was the Daruma-ji Temple in Kitakatsuragi. Founded in 613, this particular temple was believed to have been linked to a legend of a prince and a beggar. Before the existence of Daruma-ji, Prince Shōtoku was said to have met a beggar who was lying helplessly on the side of a road. Looking at the beggar, the prince decided to ask for his name, but the only response he received was complete silence. The beggar then claimed that he was dealing with extreme starvation. The prince, who was known for his compassion and selflessness, offered the starving beggar some food, drink, and a piece of his own clothing. The beggar, however, died shortly after, and Prince Shōtoku decided to give him a proper burial. A few days later, Prince Shōtoku returned to the very same spot where the beggar had been buried, but to the prince's surprise, his tomb was empty. He then noticed a piece of clothing that he had lent to the beggar earlier. It was perfectly folded and lying on the empty coffin. This mysterious event led many to believe that the beggar was, in fact, a reincarnation of Daruma Daishi, an important monk in Japanese Buddhism. After this incident, Prince Shōtoku built the Daruma-ji Temple at the same location as the tomb to honor the Buddhist figure.

Throughout his life, Prince Shōtoku was believed to have built a total of forty-six Buddhist temples and monasteries in Japan. Most of them not only served as places of worship but also as hospitals and places of lectures.

The Last Years of Prince Shōtoku's Life

In 620, Prince Shōtoku was believed to have worked with Soga no Umako to compile a collection of Japanese history. These compilations were known as *Kokki* (the "Record of the Nation") and *Tennōki* (the "Record of the Emperors"). Not much is known about these two records, except that they were later entrusted to the Soga clan. The *Tennōki* was completely destroyed years after it was compiled; this happened when Soga no Emishi committed suicide by burning his entire residence after hearing the news of his son's assassination. Although archaeologists reportedly found the remains of Soga no Emishi's burnt residence back in 2005, there was no sign of the ancient record. The *Kokki*, on the other hand, was saved from the fire by a person named Fune no Fubitoesaka, and it was later given to Prince Naka no Ōe.

Two years after the compilation of Japanese history, Prince Shōtoku fell ill. He passed away peacefully in his residence. He was only forty-eight years old. His family and the entire population of Japan grieved his death. An account in the *Nihon Shoki* says that everyone lamented the prince's death until their weeping echoed throughout the streets. No one was able to eat, as their appetite was replaced with ultimate sadness. The old cried as if they had lost their dearest child, while the young wept as if they had just witnessed their parents' passing. Even farmers let go of their hoes, spades, and sickles to wipe the tears from their gloomy faces. Everyone knew they had lost a great soul, but although Prince Shōtoku could no longer be seen walking the earth, his legacy lives on. His name is forever immortalized.

The Fate of Prince Shōtoku's Family

Since polygamy was the norm back in ancient Japan, especially among the elites and nobles, Prince Shōtoku was believed to have married more than one woman. Some sources suggested that he had at least four wives, with some of them being descendants of Empress Suiko and Soga no Umako's daughter. Prince Shōtoku's most well-known wife was named Kashiwade no Hokikimi no Iratsume, and she died a day before the prince. She was buried in the same mausoleum as her beloved husband.

It is uncertain how many children the prince had, but the most prominent one was his eldest, Prince Yamashiro. When Empress Suiko finally passed away, the Chrysanthemum Throne was yet again in dire need of a new ruler since she did not name a successor, although she did call upon Prince Yamashiro and Prince Tamura (the grandson of Emperor Bidatsu) to give them some advice. So, again, another dispute arose within the imperial court; Prince Yamashiro had all the rights to claim the throne, but so did Prince Tamura. The latter, however, gained the support of Soga no

Emishi. To solve the dispute, an attack led by Soga no Iruka was carried out on Prince Yamashiro's residence, which resulted in the prince and his family committing suicide. This marked the end of Prince Shōtoku's bloodline, at least as far as we know.

Prince Shōtoku in the Modern World

Prince Shōtoku's tomb can be found in Taishi, a small town in Osaka, which is also where the remains of several emperors and their families were buried, such as Emperor Bidatsu, Kōtoku, and Yōmei. Once the news of Prince Shōtoku's death spread throughout the Japanese archipelago, Empress Suiko immediately instructed her subjects to build Eifuku-ji, a temple that could protect the prince's tomb. The temple, however, was burned down in the late 16th century, but most of the buildings were reconstructed afterward. Enshrined statues of the prince can be found in many of the temple's halls.

Prince Shōtoku's tomb is located at the end of the temple complex, and it has been visited by many important Buddhist monks over the years. Of course, like many other mausoleums of powerful figures in Japan, visitors are not allowed to enter the tomb and can only view it from a distance.

We can also find a great number of institutions named after the prince, such as the Shōtoku Gakuen University, Seitoku Junior College of Nutrition, and Seitoku University in Matsudo. His portraits were featured on Japanese yen, and many of his sculptures and paintings have survived. One of the most famous ones is a 13th-century sculpture of the prince when he was two years old. This sculpture was discovered in 1936 and is now safely housed in the Harvard Arts Museum (Cambridge, Massachusetts, USA). Interestingly, a number of sacred items were found stashed within the sculpture's body. Some of them were writings of prayers and poems and smaller sculptures.

An old sculpture of Prince Shōtoku at the age of two.

A special ceremony is held once a century to honor the prince. The ceremony is normally held at Hōryū-ji, the same temple founded by Prince Shōtoku himself, and it is often filled with many monks, musicians, and visitors. Ancient music is played throughout the ceremony, with various traditional dances accompanying the tunes.

It is safe to say that Prince Shōtoku's name will continue to echo throughout every corner of Japan. Some might say that certain parts of his life were only a myth, while others believe that he was extraordinarily gifted. But most would agree that Prince Shōtoku was a prominent figure in ancient Japan and that his contributions played a great role in shaping the nation.

Chapter 10 – The Taika Reforms of 645 CE

With the assassination of Soga no Iruka and the death of Soga no Emishi, the Yamato Kingdom could finally break free from their monopolistic power. Prince Naka no Ōe and his conspirator, Nakatomi no Kamatari, might have been able to let out a huge sigh of relief due to their success in overthrowing the Soga clan, but Empress Kōgyoku could not relax. The empress, who was also the mother of Prince Naka no Ōe, was shocked when the news about the two Soga leaders' deaths reached her, especially since one of them was murdered right in front of her throne. So, the empress decided to renounce her position as sovereign and urged her son, Prince Naka no Ōe, to replace her. Although it was an honor to be offered such a high position, the prince refused to take the position of emperor since he knew that after the Isshi Incident, all eyes were on him. He did not want the people to think that he slew Soga no Iruka because of his desire for the Chrysanthemum Throne. Thus, he passed the offer to his uncle, who soon became Emperor Kōtoku.

With Emperor Kōtoku installed on the throne in 645, a new era in Japan was born. The Taika era (also known as the era of great change) was proclaimed by the emperor himself, along with Prince Naka no Ōe and Nakatomi no Kamatari. It was Japan's first named era in history. While Naka no Ōe's uncle wore the crown, the prince stepped in as the nation's crown prince. Nakatomi no Kamatari, on the other hand, was appointed as Naidaijin, or the Interior Minister. With this new system, both the titles of Ōmuraji and Ōomi were abolished. They were replaced with the positions of Udaijin (Minister of the Right) and Sadaijin (Minister of the Left). The emperor also appointed two monks in the imperial court to serve as state scholars. These titles were given to Takamuko no Kuromaro and Minabuchi no Shōan, both of whom had traveled to China for a diplomatic mission in 608. The two stayed in China for over three decades and brought back valuable knowledge of political law and culture from the Asian mainland.

Taika Reforms

Modeled after Tang China, the Taika reforms were a set of doctrines established by Prince Naka no Ōe and Nakatomi no Kamatari. While they wished to unite Japan, extinguish corruption, and maintain an orderly and fair government system, the Taika reforms' main purpose was to exert the emperor's dominion throughout Japan and minimize the clan leaders' excessive power. In addition to the two state scholars, four articles were developed as part of the reforms:

I. The Abolishment of Private Land Ownership and the Kabane System

The central government introduced a new system called Kochi Komin sei, which directly translates to the public land system. Through this newly introduced system, clan leaders and members of the imperial family were no longer able to possess their own lands and subjects—they belonged to the state. Prince Naka no Ōe volunteered and surrendered his lands and estates to the government. The others followed in his footsteps and did the same thing.

The hereditary kabane titles, such as Ōmuraji and Ōomi, were no longer in use. Instead, the emperor was the only person who could grant titles and lands to someone. Those who served in the court as bureaucrats were also given a type of salary called Jikifu by the central government.

II.   The Establishment of Provincial Governing Offices

The Japanese archipelago was divided into 66 imperial provinces and 592 counties. Instead of a single clan member, each province was overseen by a governor. Guardsmen called the sakimori were placed in the outer provinces, and post stations complete with stables and horses were constructed. These horses would be used by the guards across the country, especially if there was an urgent need to deliver messages and information.

III.   Census Records

Under this article, the government was to conduct a census and keep records of not only the population but also information and data about land use. Rice cultivating lands known as kubunden were redistributed to every person across the country. They had to farm these lands and pay taxes to the government.

IV.   Introduction to the New Tax System

The previous tax systems imposed by the local clan leaders in their respective territories were completely abolished and replaced with a uniform tax system called soyocho. This new system required all subjects to pay taxes in the form of rice and local specialty products. Later on, another tax system was introduced known as zoyo, which was paid in the form of conscripted labor. The number of days for mandatory labor differed according to the person's age. It was fifteen days for males aged between seventeen and twenty, thirty days for males older than sixty years old, and sixty days for those aged between twenty-one and sixty.

The reforms, of course, were not implemented as soon as it was established, but Prince Naka no Ōe's true aim was crystal clear; he wanted to unite the nation under a centralized government, allowing the emperor to hold absolute power over the nation.

Emperor Kōtoku's Death

When the emperor first rose to power, which was only two days after the Isshi Incident, he commissioned the construction of a new city in Naniwa (now known as Osaka). The capital was then moved to the new city under the order of Emperor Kōtoku. The emperor even sent diplomatic envoys to Tang China eight years after he ascended the throne, but most of the ships were said to have been lost at sea.

In the same year, however, the relationship between the emperor and the crown prince began to deteriorate. Prince Naka no Ōe had requested the emperor to move the capital back to the Yamato Province, but the emperor disagreed. Not taking no for an answer, the prince decided to move out of the current capital with many of his supporters and court courtiers. Emperor Kōtoku's wife, Empress Hashihito, was also said to have moved out of Naniwa. The emperor, who was now living in an almost empty palace, finally succumbed to illness in 654. The reactions of his subjects were unknown, although the *Nihon Shoki* describes the emperor as a gentle king, so it is likely some tears were shed. There was another vacancy on the throne. Many expected the crown prince would ascend next, but it was actually his mother who took the mantle, this time around under the name Empress Saimei.

The Battle of Baekgang

The three kingdoms of Korea had been engaged in wars with each other for over six centuries. Goguryeo owned a lot of territories in the north of the Korean Peninsula, and its people were known for their military prowess. Baekje, on the other hand, was well known for its wealth since it controlled the trade route between Korea, China, and Japan. The last kingdom of the three, Silla, was said to be the weakest among them. However, it finally formed an alliance with a powerful force in 650 and unexpectedly turned the tide of the centuries-long war.

The Kingdom of Silla first saw an opportunity to take control of the peninsula with the news of a newly formed dynasty in China. Silla formed an alliance with the Tang dynasty, which was already in a vicious rivalry with the Kingdom of Goguryeo. The joint forces raised their troops and successfully invaded Baekje in 660. The king was captured in the aftermath of the invasion. Baekje attempted to resist, but it failed terribly. However, another resistance movement was created, and this time around, the rebels sent messages to Japan, requesting military assistance to drive the united forces of Tang and Silla back to where they had started.

The call for help reached Empress Saimei, and she hastily gave orders to her subjects to prepare for a massive war. She even left the capital to oversee the preparation herself. Along with Prince Naka no Ōe, the mother and son duo began raising many troops and oversaw the construction of many warships. Japan had a close tie with Baekje—the kingdom played a great role in Japan's development—so the Japanese were not planning on laying low while the Korean kingdom was facing destruction.

The empress wished to lead the military expedition, but it never came true, as she passed away the following year. Nevertheless, in October 663, a total of 800 warships and 42,000 troops were sent by the Yamato Kingdom to face the forces of the Tang dynasty, which consisted of only 170 ships and 13,000 army troops. The Japanese troops, which most likely already imagined their victory due to their bigger numbers, launched an attack on the Tang forces at least three times in a day. The Tang army, which was led by extremely disciplined generals, managed to hold their position every single time despite being outnumbered.

The attack went on for so long that it finally exhausted the Yamato troops, opening an opportunity for the Tang forces to launch their counterattack. In just a snap of a finger, many of the Japanese ships sank into the deep water while the rest burned in bright flames. While many had fallen off their ships and drowned, a great Yamato general named Echi no Takutsu fought valiantly. He was believed to have cut down dozens of his enemies in close combat before death came knocking at his door. Near the end of the war, at least four hundred Japanese ships had reached the bottom of the sea, and ten thousand Japanese soldiers had perished. The war was, no doubt, one of the most devastating events that the Yamato Kingdom had ever been involved in.

The Kingdom of Baekje completely fell apart, and Goguryeo soon surrendered to the joint forces of Silla and Tang China. The Baekje nobles who escaped to Japan were absorbed into the Yamato court, while the commoners who made it to the archipelago served as professional artisans. As for the Japanese themselves, they began to work day and night under the order of their emperor to fortify their lands in case Silla or Tang ever shifted their focus to Japan. However, some historians claim that these fortification projects were completed mostly by Baekje refugees. The fortification projects went on for years and only stopped in 701 when the people finally realized that Silla and Tang had broken their alliance and turned on each other.

The Jinshin War

After Empress Saimei's death in August 661, Prince Naka no Ōe finally sat on the throne, going by the name of Emperor Tenji. He reigned over Japan for eleven years, but he did manage to implement some parts of the Taika reforms that he had developed. The emperor successfully conducted Japan's first national census and compiled a collection of law codes named Omi-Ryo. Consisting of a total of twenty-two volumes of administrative codes, the Omi-Ryo was considered by historians to be the first-ever Japanese legal code. However, many historians doubt its existence. Aside from the fact that archaeologists have been unable to find physical evidence of its existence, the collection of laws was not described in the *Nihon Shoki* and was mentioned only briefly in *Tōshi Kaden*, a historical record of the Fujiwara clan written between the 8th and 9th centuries.

One of the few people that the emperor never forgot was, of course, Nakatomi no Kamatari, his most loyal friend and ally. Nakatomi no Kamatari continued to support his friend until he drew his last breath. To honor his service and loyalty, Emperor Tenji granted him the rank of Taishōkan and a new family name, Fujiwara. Nakatomi passed away on November 14th, 669. The emperor drew his last breath three years later.

However, to avoid more political turmoil from appearing in the imperial court, Emperor Tenji had named his successor before his death. During his early years as emperor, he was said to have written his brother's name, Prince Ōama, as his successor; he was even appointed as crown prince. The emperor lacked a suitable son who could take his place, and most of his children were born to mothers who came from lower-ranking families. So, the only possible candidate for the throne was Prince Ōama. But eventually, Emperor Tenji happened to welcome another son named Prince Ōtomo into his family. As his favorite son grew older, the emperor soon began to change his mind about his successor. By 671, Emperor Tenji had bestowed upon his son the rank of Daijō-daijin and soon showed signs of an obsession to put Prince Ōtomo on the throne and continue his legacy. This sudden change most likely worried Prince Ōama and affected his relationship with the emperor.

Word had been going around saying that Prince Ōama could be in danger. When this rumor reached the prince's ears, he immediately resigned from the imperial court and informed the emperor of his wish to become a monk and leave the political world behind. Prince Ōama began his journey and traveled to the secluded parts of the mountains in Yoshino. The prince brought along his sons and one of his many wives, Princess Unonosarara, with him.

The months passed, and Emperor Tenji finally died of illness in January 672. With that, his twenty-four-year-old son ascended to the throne and changed his name to Emperor Kōbun.

Although Prince Ōama and his family adjusted to living in the mountains as best they could, another rumor kept the prince awake at night. The rumor said that the current emperor refused to sit still as long as he knew that Prince Ōama was alive and well. Suspecting that Emperor Kōbun might have already cooked up a plot to end his life, Prince Ōama gathered his allies and made preparations for war. This war is known as the Jinshin War, and it was the biggest one to explode in pre-modern Japan.

After sending messengers to both Ise and Iga Provinces in the east to rally the clan leaders to his side, Prince Ōama then instructed a portion of his army to march to the north and block a major route. This was done to make sure that Emperor Kōbun could never gather allies from the northern provinces. While Prince Ōama had already gained the support of the provinces in the north and the east, Emperor Kōbun sent word to the clan leaders in Kibi and Tsukushi. His hope, however, was immediately crushed, as the governor of Tsukushi refused to aid him, claiming that they could not leave their posts in case of any threats arriving from the Asian mainland.

The war took place in various locations in central Japan, with Prince Ōama emerging victorious each time. The last battle was fought on the Seta-no-Karahashi Bridge, and it was won yet again by Prince Ōama. The young emperor saw his soldiers lying lifeless on the ground, and he immediately lost hope. Emperor Kōbun had only ruled Japan for eight months, but he soon committed suicide, leaving the door open for his uncle to step in and finally take the throne.

Emperor Tenmu

After defeating his nephew, Prince Ōama ascended to the throne in 673 and gained the name Emperor Tenmu. The first thing he did as a sovereign was pretty much the same as the other emperors: he moved the capital. Since the Japanese believed in the concept of purification, it became a priority for a newly ascended emperor to move his capital to another region since the previous capital was considered impure. And so, the capital was moved back to Asuka.

New governing systems were established during Tenmu's reign, although most of them did not stray far from the Taika reforms. Instead of appointing new officials to serve as his ministers, Emperor Tenmu employed his own sons in the imperial court, while his wife carried the title of empress. A new kabane system called Yakusa no Kabane was established, and it consisted of a total of eight new kabane titles, with some of them being even higher than the previous titles of Ōmuraji and Ōomi. These titles are Mahito, Asomi, Sukune, and Imiki, and they were bestowed only upon those in the top tier. With the change in the governing structure completed, the emperor then shifted his focus to constructing another capital, which was located to the north of Asuka. Influenced by the organized arrangement of the capital in China, Emperor Tenmu's new capital, Fujiwara-kyō, was built according to the Chinese-style grid plan.

Unfortunately, despite the emperor's ambitious plans, he never got to see his new capital, as he passed away on October 1st, 686.

The throne passed to his wife, Empress Jito, who proceeded to oversee the completion of Fujiwara-kyō before finally moving the capital there.

Art and Culture

The culture during this time was referred to as the Hakuho culture, and many of its architectural designs and the arts were heavily influenced by Tang China. A small portion was indirectly influenced by Gupta art in India; the latter can be seen in the exquisite wall paintings found in the kondo (Golden Hall) of the Hōryū-ji Temple. They bear a striking resemblance to the old murals found in the Ajanta Caves, Buddhist rock-cut cave monuments in India.

Painting on the ceiling of the Ajanta Caves, India.
Source: Piyal chatterjee, CC BY-SA 4.0 https://creativecommons.org/licenses/by-sa/4.0 via Wikimedia Commons: https://commons.wikimedia.org/wiki/File:Life_circle_of_Lord_Buddha_-_A_marvel_of_painting_inside_Ajanta_Cave.jpg

A mural in the Golden Hall of Hōryū-ji.
https://commons.wikimedia.org/wiki/File:Amidhaba_paradise_Horyuji_Mural.JPG

More and more temples emerged as the years went by; historians claim that over a hundred temples and monasteries were built in this period alone, especially when Buddhism began experiencing rapid growth throughout the archipelago. The Hōryū-ji Temple, which had first been commissioned by Prince Shōtoku, was reconstructed around this time due to a lightning incident that affected almost every part of the temple complex. The Kawara-dera and Daikandai-ji were some of the new Buddhist temples constructed during this period, and they all featured some magnificent touches influenced by the architectural designs of Tang China.

Before his death, Emperor Tenmu commissioned a beautiful temple called Yakushiji to be constructed in Fujiwara-kyō, though it was later relocated to Nara. It was said that the emperor was devastated upon learning that his wife had fallen terribly ill. He began to pray to the Buddha of healing, Yakushi Nyorai, and decided to establish a temple in the deity's honor. Emperor Tenmu never got to see the finished temple, but his wife continued the project and oversaw its completion.

Yakushiji Temple in Nara.
https://commons.wikimedia.org/wiki/File:Yakushiji_panomara.jpg

Considered to be one of the most beautiful temples to ever exist in Japan, the Yakushiji's famous features were the symmetrical layout and the two finely constructed pagodas accompanying each side of the main hall. Unfortunately, in 973, a fire engulfed most of the temple's structure, which was followed by another fire in 1528 that destroyed the main hall. However, massive reconstruction projects were arranged in the 20th century. The only original structure of the temple that still stands today is the three-story East Pagoda.

Aside from the fine architectural designs seen in temples and the flourishing poetry brought by the Baekje aristocrats who came to Japan after the fall of their kingdom, funerals during this period also began to see some changes. Buddhist-style cremation funerals became more popular, especially when the government restricted the construction of massive burial mounds. Thus, the number of new kofun tombs began to drop drastically until they completely disappeared.

Chapter 11 – Tōdai-ji and the Bronze Buddha

Tōdai-ji (the "Eastern Great Temple") is one of the Buddhist temples constructed during the ancient Nara period that still stands today. Initially commissioned by Emperor Shōmu in 728, the great temple was actually built as an appeasement for the troubled spirit of Prince Motoi, the emperor's late son.

Prince Motoi was born to Emperor Shōmu and Empress Kōmyō in November 727. He was the emperor's first son, and he was appointed as the nation's crown prince at the age of thirty-two days, which was a rare occurrence, although there was not yet a minimum age in place for an appointment in the imperial court. Unfortunately, despite his parents' joy and tender care, the infant crown prince fell terribly sick and passed away shortly after. He was less than a year old when his remains were buried on Mount Naho.

With the crown prince's death, the imperial court had lost their next heir to the throne. To make matters worse, a rumor spread, suggesting that the late crown prince's mysterious sickness and death were actually caused by some kind of magic by Prince Nagaya, who served the court as Sadaijin at the time. He was the next possible successor to the Chrysanthemum Throne. So, the emperor, who was still in mourning over his only son, began to distrust Nagaya. Without strong evidence, the Fujiwara Four (the sons of Fujiwara no Fuhito) took matters into their own hands; they pressed charges against Prince Nagaya and forced him to commit suicide. His wife and children were killed at the same time. Prince Nagaya's death was believed to have started a curse, as the Japanese archipelago was then overwhelmed by several terrible incidents in the next following years.

Six years after the slander and death of Prince Nagaya, the Japanese archipelago was struck with a smallpox epidemic. Beginning in a city in Northern Kyushu, the illness was said to have plagued a Japanese fisherman who had returned to the archipelago after being stranded in the Korean Peninsula. From there, the plague spread throughout Northern Kyushu, leading to many deaths. Crops failed to grow, and agricultural activities drastically decreased. Famine greatly affected the people, and the economy declined.

By 736, several officials from the imperial court had passed through the infected area in Northern Kyushu. As a result, the party was immediately infected. While some of them perished, the remaining officials returned to the capital, thus spreading the disease to Nara. By 737, the plague had slowed down. It was reported that nearly 35 percent of Japan's population had died of smallpox, including the Fujiwara Four, who had driven Prince Nagaya and his family to their deaths.

The disaster, however, did not stop after the terrible plague. Emperor Shōmu's kingdom was yet again in chaos when Fujiwara no Hirotsugu started a rebellion against the government. However, Fujiwara no Hirotsugu claimed that his war was only with Kibi no Makibi and Genbo, who, according to Hirotsugu himself, was the reason the Fujiwara clan's influence in the court had been suppressed. The rebellion was successfully handled by the government's forces. Hirotsugu was captured and killed, and his supporters were imprisoned, flogged, and exiled.

Emperor Shōmu somehow believed that he was the one responsible for all the terrors happening in his kingdom. And so, he began to show signs of becoming a devout Buddhist; he believed that the nation could be cleansed, saved, and protected by Buddhism. In 741, he issued an edict that required the construction of a temple in all sixty-six provinces of Japan, as well as the construction of Tōdai-ji's Great Buddha Hall. This would come to house the colossal bronze Buddha known as Daibutsu. To make sure the project went well, a Buddhist priest named Gyoku traveled throughout the entire archipelago seeking donations. Over two million people provided wood, metal, cloth, and rice. The priest also returned with at least three hundred thousand laborers who would later work on the bronze Buddha and its great hall. Although the emperor himself had provided financial support for the construction from his royal coffers, the construction of these temples, especially the Tōdai-ji, nearly led the Japanese state into bankruptcy. Special taxes were imposed on everyone to ensure the completion of Tōdai-ji, which caused many to suffer, including those in the higher social classes.

Although the Tōdai-ji Temple was commissioned as early as 728, it was not actually opened until about twenty-four years later. Standing at the east of the palace, the Tōdai-ji was made the provincial temple of Yamato Province after the issuing of an edict (kokubunji) by Emperor Shōmu. It also served as the headquarters for the other provincial temples in the archipelago. It housed offices for all six Buddhist schools in Japan: Hosso, Kegon, Jōjitsu, Sanron, Ritsu, and Kusha. Other than being a place of worship, the temple was used as a learning center; it featured both a college and a library, which were often used by monks and priests to translate Buddhist sutras. The Tōdai-ji was also the very first Buddhist temple to install an image of the Shinto kami of war and culture,

Hachiman, as it was believed that the kami had the ultimate ability to protect the sacred temple.

Daibutsu, the Largest Bronze Buddha in the World

Daibutsuden, the Great Buddha Hall of Tōdai-ji.

The Tōdai-ji Temple was indeed built to impress, despite the project first being commissioned by the emperor as a means to protect the kingdom against chaos. At the center of the temple complex, one could find the grand hondō or the main hall named Daibutsuden (the Great Buddha Hall). In this very hall, the largest bronze Buddha statue in the whole wide world stood. Measuring almost fifteen meters (forty-nine feet) tall and weighing at least five hundred tons, this sitting Buddha statue was a representation of Dainichi Nyorai (also known as Vairocana), one of the most important Buddhas in the Kegon sect. The Buddha statue sits on top of a bronze lotus pedestal with his right hand raised, which symbolizes a gesture of teaching. The Buddha's snail-curled hair is said to have been made out of 966 bronze spheres, while the base of the lotus pedestal features the unique engravings of *Rengezō sekai,* also known as the Lotus Treasury World. By the Buddha's sides are two of his bodhisattvas; on his left is the bodhisattva, Kokuzo Bosatsu, which was built in the early 18th century.

The bronze Buddha of Tōdai-ji (Nara Daibutsu).

The construction of the Buddha statue took a few years to complete. The first construction site was in Shigaraki, and it was later moved to Nara after the emperor relocated the capital back to Heijō-kyō. After the completion of the years-long construction, an "Eye-Opening Ceremony" was held in 752 to consecrate the image of the Vairocana Buddha. Overseen by Empress Kōken, the ceremony was attended by nearly ten thousand monks and four thousand dancers from the Asian mainland. At that time, it was considered the largest international event ever held in East Asia. The retired Emperor Shōmu and his consort, Kōmyō, were also among the respected guests of the ceremony.

Music filled the air, which was followed by several dance performances by dancers from Korea and China. When it was finally time to enshrine the newly constructed Buddha statue, the officiating monk, who was a respected Indian priest named Bodhisena, painted the pupils of the Buddha by using a special brush named *kaigan kuyo-e*, thus imbuing the Buddha with life. Then, former Emperor Shōmu was believed to have sat in front of the Buddha and made a vow to completely devote himself to the Three Treasures of Buddhism: the Buddha, the Dharma (Buddhist law), and the Sangha (the Buddhist monastic community).

In 855, slightly over a century after the completion of the statue's construction, an earthquake struck the Japanese archipelago, destroying a part of the bronze Daibutsu. Its massive head fell to the ground. The statue, however, was restored under the order of the central government soon afterward. When one of Japan's biggest conflicts, the Genpei War, exploded in 1180, the statue was once again destroyed. The leader of the Taira clan instructed his men to torch the complex since the Buddhist monks showed their support to the clan's worst rival, the Minamoto. Unlike the damage done by the earthquake centuries before, the Genpei War seriously damaged the Tōdai-ji complex. Not only did it severely destroy the massive Buddha image, but it also caused heavy casualties.

The Taira clan destroyed another temple during this time, but the imperial government could focus on restoring one temple at a time since it was drowning in financial problems. And so, the constructions of the Tōdai-ji and the Daibutsu were prioritized. Under the supervision of former Emperor Go-Shirakawa, a restoration project was launched. The former emperor appointed an obscure monk named Chōgen to travel across the Japanese lands and collect funds to ensure the restoration project ran smoothly. The monk was believed to have devoted over twenty years of his life working on the restoration of the Daibutsu and other important structures of the Tōdai-ji.

The project continued even after the end of the Genpei War. Under the supervision of the victorious Minamoto, Tōdai-ji was finally restored in 1195. However, due to some financial difficulties, the temple was built on a smaller scale compared to the original.

Since Japan is situated on the Pacific Ring of Fire, it is not surprising that Japan was hit by yet another terrible earthquake in 1709, resulting in the destruction of the Great Buddha Hall. It was rebuilt soon after, and it still stands in Nara Prefecture today. Just as before, the reconstruction of the hall was costly. Because of that, the hall was reconstructed on a smaller scale; it measured about 57 meters (187 feet) long and 48 meters (157 feet) tall. Nevertheless, the hall is still named the largest wooden building in the world today.

Other Structures at Tōdai-ji

As one of the largest temple complexes in Japan, the Tōdai-ji comprises several other magnificent structures. The main gate of the temple, known as Nandaimon ("The Great South Gate"), measured at least twenty-one meters (sixty-nine feet) long and features an impressive double hip-and-gable roof—an architectural design popular during the Kamakura period. Although the gate was first constructed in the Nara period, it was, unfortunately, destroyed by a typhoon several years later. However, thanks to the reconstruction project launched in the early 12th century, the gate still exists today.

A wooden sculpture of one of the Niō guardians that protect the temple complex from evil spirits.

Lisa Beké, CC BY 3.0 https://creativecommons.org/licenses/by/3.0 via Wikimedia Commons: https://commons.wikimedia.org/wiki/File:20100716_Nara_Todaiji_Nandaimon_2252.jpg

To protect the temple from being infested with evil spirits and demons, two wooden sculptures of Niō guardians measuring eight meters (twenty-six feet) tall were added in 1203 CE. About four years after the construction of the Niō guardians, a 12th-century Zen priest named Yōsai added an exquisite bell tower called Shoro to the temple complex. The structure houses the second largest bell in Japan, and it weighs over twenty-six tons.

Shoro, which houses the second largest bell in Japan.

To the west of the Great Buddha Hall stands the Nigatsu-dō (the "Hall of the Second Month"). First erected in the 8th century, the hall is where the Omizutori, the sacred water-drawing festival, takes place every second month of the lunar calendar (around March 1st until March 14th). Since the hall is located on top of a hill, one can feast their eyes on breathtaking views from there.

To the south of Nigatsu-dō is another grand hall known as the Hokke-dō (the "Lotus Hall"). Just like the Nigatsu-dō, Hokke-dō was founded in the 8th century. The structure features two separate halls: the worship hall and the image hall. The latter, which houses an impressive collection of Buddhist statues, appears to be darker than the other since minimal light is allowed to shine through. This is to ensure all of the 8th-century statues remain well preserved. While the 3.6-meter (12-foot) statue of Fukukenjaku Kannon is the highlight of Hokke-dō's image hall, there is another unique clay sculpture hidden away from visitors. The statue of Shūkongōjin is only made available for viewing once a year (every December 16th), and because of this extreme preservation measure, the sculpture is said to have maintained its original state. The shape is as exquisite as ever, and not a single color has faded.

Statue of Fukukenjaku Kannon inside the Hokke-dō.

Chapter 12 – The Nara Period Explained

The Nara period took place in 710 when the capital was moved to Heijō-kyō, Nara. The Nara period lasted for slightly over eighty years, and writing exploded during this time. The *Kojiki* and *Nihon Shoki*, two of the most important written records of Japanese history, were finally compiled. The *Kojiki*, which was commissioned by Empress Genmei in 712, features the story of the imperial court during its early days up until the reign of Empress Suiko, as well as various religious practices and ceremonies held during ancient times. The record, however, is considered semi-historical since most accounts are fused with legends and myths. The same could also be said about the *Nihon Shoki*, although it contains a more detailed account of ancient Japanese history. Initially commissioned by Emperor Tenmu during his reign, the *Nihon Shoki* was written in classical Chinese and tells the story of how the world was shaped, followed by accounts of dozens of emperors—both legendary and historical—and various events that took place until the 8th century.

Beautiful works of poetry also began to appear during the Nara period. Ōtomo no Yakamochi, a government official and poet, was believed to have compiled 4,516 different poems into a collection called Man'yōshū. While his own works were also included in the collection, some of the poems were written by emperors, nobles, and even court ladies.

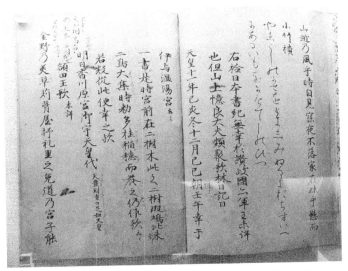

A page of the Man'yōshū, which is kept in the Tokyo National Museum.

Japan also maintained its international relations. Diplomatic envoys or *kentōshi* were sent to Tang China every twenty years. More knowledge and cultural influences were brought back, and several of the students who returned from the Asian mainland were promoted to high ranks in the Yamato court. The Japanese archipelago also accepted many visitors from other parts of the world, ranging from India to Vietnam, Indonesia, and Malaysia. When foreign visitors arrived at the main gates of the kingdom, they were often welcomed with grand ceremonies filled with music and dance performances.

Although great art and literature were some of the prominent features of the Nara period, the life of the commoners only slightly improved. While the elites lived lavishly in their estates, the lower classes were still plagued by poverty, and most of them still lived in rural villages. They supported themselves with agricultural activities, though their technology remained the same as in previous periods. Shintoism was widely practiced by the commoners, while the nobles held strong beliefs in Buddhism, especially Emperor Shōmu, who was known for issuing the massive construction of the bronze Buddha, which almost dried out the nation's wealth.

The Aftermath of Emperor Tenmu's Death

Right after Emperor Tenmu's death, the Japanese archipelago was ruled by his wife, Empress Jito, although she did not rise to the throne officially at this time. The empress was said to have been a great ruler, something she had already demonstrated before her husband's death. But Empress Jito did not plan to rule for too long, which could be the reason she did not officially take the throne. The empress was actually planning to install her own son, Prince Kusakabe, on the Chrysanthemum Throne.

Ever since he was young, the prince was groomed by his royal parents to become an emperor. He was absorbed into the imperial court at a young age and was taught how to handle administrative work. He was also appointed as crown prince during his father's reign. Empress Jito was, no doubt, confident that her son would be a great fit for the throne. However, one problem kept her awake at night; Prince Kusakabe had some health issues.

Later, another contender surfaced and began to quickly gain support from the other officials in the Yamato court. His name was Prince Ōtsu, and he was also the son of Emperor Tenmu. Described as a modest man who had a good physique and was very skillful in sword fights and martial arts, Prince Ōtsu gained favor from many, from those working in the ministry office to the peasants working the lands. We could say that everyone liked him—everyone except for Empress Jito.

While everyone was enthralled by Prince Ōtsu's polite manners, Empress Jito saw him as an obstacle. Word soon reached the empress, informing her that Prince Ōtsu was quietly planning a rebellion. Not wanting to miss this golden opportunity to get rid of him, the empress charged Prince Ōtsu with treason. He was immediately captured and killed at his residence; some claimed he was forced to commit suicide. But was Prince Ōtsu really planning a rebellion? Or was it actually a plan devised by the empress? We may never know for sure.

Nevertheless, the empress had successfully removed the obstacle, leaving a clear way for her beloved son to step up as emperor. Unfortunately, her effort was for nothing, as Prince Kusakabe soon died of his illness. With her son gone, Empress Jito had no other choice but to take the mantle and rule the kingdom officially.

Continuing her late husband's work, Empress Jito moved the capital to Fujiwara-kyō after the city's completion. The new capital was the first one to be used by three consecutive rulers, breaking the old tradition of capitals being moved every time a new emperor took the throne. The empress oversaw the completion of many temples, especially the Yakushi-ji. A new law code was enacted under her reign, and another census was conducted. Since social classes became even more important during this era, the records obtained from the census were considered valuable; the government could now keep track of everyone's lineage and bloodline. From this point on, a census had to be conducted once every six years.

Later on, Empress Jito would abdicate her throne in favor of her grandson, who was the son of Prince Kusakabe. He rose to the throne as Emperor Monmu in 697. Influenced by Tang China and realizing the idea of the Taika reforms, the new emperor established the Taihō-ritsuryō (Code of Taihō) in 701. It included both punishment and administrative laws. The government was also improved and transformed into a much more organized structure, with two offices placed right under the emperor himself, followed by eight different ministries. Each of these positions was filled by reliable chieftains and members of the imperial line.

Life under Emperor Monmu's reign

During this time, commoners still lived in villages. Most of the time, they engaged in agricultural activities to survive. Taxes were collected from them no matter their living situation. Women and slaves only had to pay a certain amount of rice, but men had to pay with rice, cloth, specialty products, and manual labor for sixty days. To make it harder on them, the villagers had to deliver their payment to the capital themselves. This could have been a long journey depending on where one lived.

Adult males were drafted for three-year periods of guard duty, where they would be sent to specific regions across the archipelago to keep an eye out for possible invasions from the Asian mainland. Although they were exempted from taxes during this time, these people still had to finance their own equipment, travel, and supplies. Due to high taxes and military drafts, there were cases of census fraud. Men would lie and register themselves as women so they could avoid the burdens placed upon them by the government.

The Rise of the Fujiwara Clan

The Fujiwara clan was founded by none other than Nakatomi no Kamatari after he gained a new surname from Emperor Tenji a couple of years before his death. Although the Fujiwara clan had long been established in the Yamato court, it rose to even greater heights when Fujiwara no Fuhito (the son of Kamatari) gained favor from Empress Jito. To further strengthen their ties with the imperial line, Fuhito married his daughter to Emperor Monmu, and they soon bore a son named Obito.

Emperor Monmu, however, only lived until the age of twenty-five. He died in 707, leaving the throne empty and ready to welcome another ruler. Of course, Fuhito was obsessed with putting his grandchild, Prince Obito, on the throne, but it was not that easy. Since his mother was not the late emperor's main consort, Obito could not claim the throne since it was prioritized to the emperor and his main consort's sons. But this did not stop Fuhito; he eventually came up with a plan that made it possible for Prince Obito to step up as the next emperor, although he did not live long enough to witness his grandson sit on the throne. The other officials in the court were no doubt unhappy with this turnaround, especially the Sadaijin, Prince Nagaya.

However, since Obito was merely a child, he was unable to rule. So, his grandmother ascended the throne as Empress Genmei and ruled until her grandson reached an age fit to govern. Under the empress's rule, the capital was moved from Fujiwara-kyō to Nara, marking the start of the Nara period. The first Japanese coins were introduced during this era. Archaeologists have found the remnants of coins older than the ones from the Nara period; however, they were probably used only in rituals and not as currency.

Rice and cloth were used as currency before coins came along. In 708, two years after the enthronement of Empress Genmei, silver and bronze coins were introduced to the public, although few agreed with the change. The nation only had a limited supply of silver, which made the production of silver coins pretty rare. Counterfeits were common, as people would often mix cheaper metals to create silver coins. Thus, the production of silver coins ended, and the government started to use bronze coins for nearly everything. Construction workers who had spent day and night building temples and shrines were paid with a certain number of bronze coins, as were the government officials. Soon, coins could even be used to exchange for a rank in the court.

The oldest Japanese bronze coin, *Wadōkaichin*.

By 707, Prince Obito had reached the age of fourteen, but Empress Genmei thought it was not the time for him to take the throne since he was still too young to handle the pressures of being an emperor. Obito was instead appointed as crown prince, and the empress herself abdicated in the following year in favor of her daughter, who became Empress Genshō. Empress Genshō ruled for nine years before she finally passed the throne to the twenty-three-year-old Prince Obito, who became Emperor Shōmu.

Fujiwara no Fuhito, on the other hand, was appointed as Udaijin, but he later died in 720. He did leave behind a legacy: his four sons, who later founded the four houses of the Fujiwara clan. With Fuhito's death, power in the court was seized by none other than Prince Nagaya. He had spent years trying to erase the Fujiwara clan's influence in the court, but he was forced to stop when Fuhito's four sons stepped in to end the rivalry once and for all. He was falsely charged with treason in 729 and forced to commit suicide. His family was also killed, and his loyal supporters were exiled. Legend has it that before committing suicide, Prince Nagaya cursed the living with misfortunes and death.

Now that Prince Nagaya was gone, the power in the court shifted yet again. It was completely dominated by Fuhito's four sons. Their methods of removing obstacles in their way were no doubt ruthless, but they did gain the public's favor. Thanks to the brothers, taxes were greatly reduced, military drafts were abolished, and more hospitals and charitable institutions were built. But, of course, the public's perception of the Fujiwaras was not the only thing that mattered. To further solidify their influence in the imperial court, their younger sister, Kōmyō, was married to Emperor Shōmu. Although Kōmyō did not have royal blood in her veins, she was later promoted to empress consort, which made it possible for her son with the emperor to take the throne in the future. With this, the Fujiwara clan had scored a huge win in the imperial court. But perhaps Fuhito's four sons really could not escape from the curse of Prince Nagaya, as they all perished when the smallpox epidemic hit Japan in 737. However, their deaths did not mean the end of the Fujiwara clan.

Conflicts, Power Struggles, and More Murders

Schemes, plague, and continuous struggles continued during the reign of Emperor Shōmu. In fact, a terrible plague had turned him into a devout Buddhist, resulting in the emperor issuing many constructions of Buddhist temples across the archipelago. Soon, the ongoing disasters and political feuds led the emperor to move the capital several times until his subjects' rejections could be heard loud enough that he returned the capital back to Nara. Emperor Shōmu finally had enough of the pressures of the political world, and he abdicated the throne in favor of his daughter, who reigned as Empress Kōken. As for Shōmu, he decided to enter the priesthood and devote his life to Buddhism.

In the imperial court, another clan rose to power after the death of Fuhito's four sons. This clan was called Tachibana, and it was led by an influential figure named Tachibana no Moroe. On the other side of the court was Fujiwara no Nakamaro, who had risen through the ranks with the help of Empress Kōken's mother, Empress Kōmyō. Unable to sit still while Moroe gained more power each day, Nakamaro dreamed of getting rid of him. One day, the officials attended a party, where Moroe accidentally expressed his comments about the current ruling empress. Seeing this incident as an opportunity, Nakamaro spread the word about Moroe starting a revolt. He then forced Moroe to resign. Moroe soon complied, as he feared his life was on the line.

The event angered Moroe's son, Tachibana no Naramaro, who planned revenge in response to his father's forced resignation. And so, he devised an ambitious strategy to take down Nakamaro and replace Empress Kōken. However, his plans turned out to be a failure before they could even begin. When Naramaro gathered allies to participate in his scheme, one of them decided to turn on him and informed high officials of his plans. Word spread faster than lightning, and he was soon questioned by the empress herself. Holding his ground, Naramaro admitted to having forged the plan and continued to criticize the government's failure as a means to justify his actions. In response, Empress Kōken exiled him, but that was not enough for Fujiwara no Nakamaro. He ordered his men to murder Naramaro, even though he had already been sentenced to exile. Some claimed that Naramaro died slowly and painfully, as Nakamaro's men had beaten him to death with wooden canes.

With Naramaro's death, Nakamaro could easily control the court. Later on, Empress Kōken stepped down. Some suggest that Nakamaro, with the help of Kōmyō, persuaded her, while others claim that the empress was ill. Nevertheless, with Empress Kōken out of the picture, Emperor Junnin was installed on the throne. The new emperor was nothing more than a puppet, as the real power was in the hands of Nakamaro and Kōmyō.

Things were going well for Nakamaro until Kōmyō suddenly passed away in 760. This opened the door for Kōken to gain the throne again. With the strong influences she had gained during her time as empress, she proclaimed that she would be the one to oversee state matters. This, of course, shocked Nakamaro, who had already begun to lose support from many of his followers. To put an end to Kōken, he started a rebellion. He gathered his own military forces and met with a fortune teller to help him decide a date for the rebellion to take place. The fortune teller, however, turned on him and informed Kōken of his plans. After rewarding the fortune teller for this information, Kōken stripped Nakamaro of all his power and positions, including his surname: Fujiwara. Nakamaro attempted an escape while trying to gather more allies, but he was soon cornered by Kōken. He was killed along with his entire family, and his remaining allies were exiled.

Emperor Junnin, on the other hand, was banished to Awaji Island, as he was charged with conspiring with Nakamaro. Some suggest that the former emperor attempted an escape but failed miserably and was assassinated. With zero obstacles lying ahead, Kōken rose to the Chrysanthemum Throne for the second time. She reigned as Empress Shōtoku with the help of a mysterious man named Dōkyō.

How Dōkyō Almost Turned Japan into a Theocracy

Who exactly was Dōkyō, and how did he manage to get on the empress's good side? Dōkyō was actually a Buddhist priest who had crossed paths with the empress when she was seriously ill. The priest was said to have saved her life; it was believed that he cured her using magical Buddhist powers. Ever since then, they became extremely close to the point that many claimed they became lovers.

Due to his close relationship with the empress, Dōkyō was able to rise through the ranks with ease. Historians believe that Dōkyō wished to change the Japanese government and convert it into a theocracy, with Buddhist priests placed on top of the pyramid instead of a single emperor. He even went to the extent of persuading the empress to make changes in the current government system so that it was more in line with Buddhist beliefs. Monks and priests started to get employed more in the imperial court. A number of lands were restricted, so the nobles could not own land without the court's permission. Instead, more land was provided to construct temples.

As the days went by, people began to worry that the empress might abdicate the throne in favor of the Buddhist priest who had no blood ties to the imperial family. To make matters worse, Dōkyō himself had started to act like a ruler of the nation; he wore clothes with the same standard as the imperial family and ate the same things they did. He even had his own special palanquin, which was only used for those with royal blood.

Later, the nation was shocked by a prediction made by an oracle from Usa Hachimangu Shrine. It was said that the kingdom would only achieve peace if Dōkyō was put on top. This sudden prediction quickly enraged many, especially since Dōkyō was not related to the imperial family. To quench the noise of her subjects, the empress sent an official to the shrine so that they could confirm the prediction. This time around, however, the oracle stated that none should ever rise to the Chrysanthemum Throne except for those who belonged to the imperial family.

So, when Empress Shōtoku died in 770, the Fujiwara clan members took matters into their own hands and immediately exiled the ambitious priest, thus saving both the imperial line and the kingdom from being transformed into a theocracy. Female royals were also prohibited from sitting on the throne—at least for eight hundred years—after this incident. As for the Fujiwara clan, this meant that their power continued to grow in the imperial court, and they would soon prosper even more during the Heian period.

Chapter 13 – The Shosoin Repository and Its Many Treasures

Ever since Buddhism arrived in the Japanese lands, temples began to adorn every corner of the archipelago. Following the completion of Asuka-dera (formerly known as Hōkō-ji), which was built as early as the late 6th century, many more temples were constructed throughout the years, each with its own uniqueness that distinguishes it from the others. Today, Japan houses over eighty thousand Buddhist temples, with the world-famous Tōdai-ji being the largest of them all.

While the Tōdai-ji was best known for its impressive grand hondō and the colossal bronze Buddha that sits inside it, the temple complex also features an 8th-century storehouse that protected many artifacts, trinkets, and documents from Japan's ancient past. The storehouse, often referred to as the Shosoin Repository, stands at the northwestern corner of the Grand Buddha Hall and has been there ever since the Nara period (710–784 CE). Although the exact date of its construction remains unknown, the Shosoin Repository's initial purpose was to store treasures belonging to the imperial family, particularly those of Emperor Shōmu and his empress consort, Kōmyō.

Front view of the Shosoin Repository.

Empress Kōmyō was first married to Shōmu in 716 when he held the title of crown prince. Kōmyō was the mother of both Empress Kōken and Prince Motoi, who died a year after his birth. The empress was believed to have embraced the Buddhist faith. It is thought that she was the one who advised the emperor to construct the Tōdai-ji following the many disasters that had terrorized the archipelago. She was also highly skilled in calligraphy; she was responsible for producing the *Gakki-ron,* one of the oldest copies of a text by Wang Xizhi, a famous Chinese calligrapher from the 4th century CE. The empress consort was also an influential political figure, as she played a prominent role alongside her husband. It is safe to assume that the imperial pair had a close relationship.

So, when Emperor Shōmu died in 755, the mourning empress consort decided to dedicate over six hundred treasures to the bronze Buddha of Tōdai-ji as an offering to ensure the spirit of her deceased husband was at peace. The offerings were done in the span of several years. To preserve the state of the treasures, they were kept within a room in the Shosoin Repository.

The storehouse itself was built using a unique Japanese architectural style called Azekura-zukuri. Resembling a sturdy log cabin, this particular style has actually been around ever since the ancient Yayoi and Kofun periods, although, back then, this kind of simple yet durable wooden cabin was typically used to store rice and other agricultural harvests. The Shosoin was made out of age-darkened cypress, which is a type of timber known for its high durability. The entire structure did not feature a single nail or bolt. The triangular wooden beams that came together in each corner of this rectangular building are what make the Shosoin so special. In fact, this construction method without nails saved the structure from being destroyed by earthquakes. While the Shosoin has gone through minor restoration processes and repairs, most of its structures remain unaltered. It witnessed a number of destructions during ancient times, including the torching of the Tōdai-ji by the Minamoto clan and the siege of Nara in the Heian period, but thanks to its durability, the storehouse is still intact and has managed to preserve almost all of its treasures.

The triangular wooden beams that come together at the corner of the structure.
ignis, CC BY-SA 3.0 http://creativecommons.org/licenses/by-sa/3.0/, via Wikimedia Commons: https://commons.wikimedia.org/wiki/File:Azekura-dukuri_JPN.JPG

Since its main purpose was to preserve centuries-old artifacts, a lot of effort was put into its construction. Only the highest quality of timber could be used to build the repository, as this would allow it to expand and contract according to the weather conditions. The storehouse measures about fourteen meters (forty-six feet) tall, and it is poised on top of forty sturdy columns so that it is raised over two meters (six feet) above the ground. The elevation was done to avoid dampness and protect the entire structure from being infested with vermin and destructive pests. The repository also features a hip-and-gable roof covered in traditional ceramic tiles; the roof has the ability to shed water and repel fire. The Shosoin also lacks stairs to prevent thieves from easily entering the storehouse. The treasures, on the other hand, were kept in elevated wooden chests made out of cedarwood. This protected the artifacts from being exposed to unnecessary light, which explains their marvelous state. Most of the precious artifacts still remain in their original states; the ancient paintings are as vibrant as ever, the exquisite fabrics are still in perfect condition, and the inks on the old manuscripts are still clearly visible.

The Treasures of the Shosoin Repository

The interior of the Shosoin Repository was separated into three parts. The Northern Room was historically reserved for all of the gifts and offerings made by Empress Kōmyō to the bronze Daibutsu. Both the middle and southern rooms were used by high-ranking Buddhist monks to store various ceremonial objects and important articles and documents belonging to the central government. This included tax records, censuses, and poetry books, with most of them originating from the 8th century.

Over the years, the repository housed over nine thousand treasures of the past, with some of them originating from different countries all over the world, such as China, kingdoms in Southeast Asia, and the Middle East. These items are divided into different categories: *Butsugu* (Buddhist objects), *Fukushoku* (clothing pieces and accessories), *Chōdo Hin* (furniture), *Yūgi Gu* (games), *Gakki* (musical instruments), and *Buji* (weaponry). Each of these items preserved in the storehouse reveals a lot about the economy of ancient Japan, as well as the social and cultural lives of the Japanese people, especially during the Nara period.

Torige ritsujyo no byōbu, an old painting preserved in the Shosoin Repository.
https://commons.wikimedia.org/wiki/File:%E9%B3%A5%E6%AF%9B%E7%AB%8B%E5%A5%B3%E5%B1%8F%E9%A2%A81.jpg

The Torige ritsujyo no byōbu, for example, is a well-preserved folding screen that features a painting of a young lady, possibly a depiction of someone from Tang China, under a tree with her flowy garments beautifully decorated with colorful bird feathers. Through this rare painting alone, we can get an insight into the feminine beauty standard of a noblewoman during the Nara period. Cut glass bowls (Hakururi no wan) possibly originated from the Middle East, and there were pitchers and cups from Persia, highly intricate musical instruments from Tang China, a silver incense burner (Odo no Gosu), ceramic drum body, lacquered ewer, and a golden Buddhist scepter (Saikaku no nyoi) made out of the horn of a rhinoceros. These items prove that ancient Japan had connections with the Silk Road.

An 8th-century incense burner.
https://commons.wikimedia.org/wiki/File:Silver_Incense_Burner_Shosoin.JPG

A lacquered ewer measuring over forty-one centimeters (sixteen inches) tall.
https://commons.wikimedia.org/wiki/File:LACQUERED_EWER_Shosoin.JPG

The most popular treasure stored in Shosoin, however, is a musical instrument called Kuwanoki no genkan. This rare lute is believed to have originated from China and is made out of mulberry wood with an inscription of the word "Todaiji" on the back of its round body. This four-string lute also features a detailed motif of three Chinese men playing Go, a traditional board game that was first made famous in China about 2,500 years ago.

Another musical instrument that survived the many centuries is the Raden Shitan no Gogen Biwa, a five-stringed biwa lute of Indian origin; the one stored in the repository is, in fact, the only one left of its kind. Almost like the Kuwanoki no genkan, this ancient biwa is adorned with a motif that depicts a man riding a camel. Made out of red sandalwood, this musical instrument is exquisitely decorated with nacre or mother-of-pearl, as well as golden and silver motifs in the shapes of birds, flowers, and trees.

Through the donations made by Empress Kōmyō as a dedication to her late husband, many of Emperor Shōmu's personal belongings survived through the years. A Buddhist robe, a fine embroidered armrest, a bronze mirror inlaid with mother-of-pearl, silk fabrics, and intricate swords are among the six hundred treasures donated by the empress consort. A sword named Kingin Denso no Karatachi was one of the emperor's most prized possessions. The hilt of the sword is made out of white sharkskin and is adorned with crystals, glass, and golden lacquer. However, its complex sheath is what makes the sword unique. It was created using a technique known as *makkinru*, and it features fine depictions of animals, along with two hanging ornaments known as *ashikanamono*.

A lacquered bronze mirror with mother-of-pearl inlays.
https://commons.wikimedia.org/wiki/File:8Lobed_Mirror_Inlay_Shosoin.jpg

Believed to have arrived in Japan from Tang China, there were initially a hundred swords made in the *makkinru* method. Most of them, however, have not been found, most likely because they were used as weapons by Fujiwara no Nakamaro in his rebellion. In 2010, two of these long-lost ancient swords were found buried underneath the pedestal of the bronze Buddha of Tōdai-ji. Out of a hundred, only three—including Kingin Denso no Karatachi—were ever discovered and safely stored in the Shosoin.

Although the Shosoin was designated as a national treasure of Japan in 1997 and was registered as a UNESCO World Heritage Site, the ancient treasures were no longer kept there by the 20th century. In 1953 and 1962, two modern repositories were built in close proximity to the Shosoin Repository; they are known today as the East Repository and West Repository. Instead of timber, these two modern structures were constructed using reinforced concrete and structural steel. To further preserve the conditions of the rare treasures, the interior of the repositories is equipped with HVAC systems. Textiles are stored in the East Repository, while most of the other treasures are kept safely in the West Repository.

The public is, of course, not allowed to enter these repositories; it is strictly sealed under the order of the imperial family. However, every autumn, the Nara National Museum holds an exhibition for the public that lasts for two weeks. It contains approximately sixty ancient treasures from the Shosoin.

Chapter 14 – The Heian Period (794–1185)

The Heian period marked its beginning when the official capital of Japan was relocated from Nara to Heian-kyō (modern-day Kyoto). Emperor Kanmu (Japan's fiftieth emperor) was the one responsible for the relocation. By the end of the Nara period, Buddhism had strongly spread its influence across the archipelago, with more and more temples filling up the central region of the capital. Noticing that their influence was spreading too fast, the emperor began to express his concern about the state of the government. He did not wish to see history repeat itself; remember, the imperial court had almost been taken over by the Buddhist priest Dōkyō many years prior. It was possible it could happen all over again. And so, in 784, Emperor Kanmu relocated the capital to Nagaokakyō.

The construction of the new capital was overseen by Fujiwara no Tanetsugu, the emperor's advisor. However, a year after the relocation, Tanetsugu was found dead, murdered by an unknown assassin. Questions were asked, and investigations were carried out, but no one had witnessed the incident. Not a single soul knew who the culprit was until shocking news reached the imperial court. Someone stepped up and claimed that the murderer was none other than Crown Prince Sawara, the emperor's younger brother. He was soon arrested, although he was adamant about his innocence. As a protest, Prince Sawara starved himself during his imprisonment until he was somehow proven guilty and sent to exile on Awaji Island. However, he never set foot on the island, as he died due to starvation on the way. After this incident, more misfortunes fell upon the state. For instance, there were deaths of the imperial family, and a terrible flood occurred. Seeing the chaotic events as a curse by his late younger brother, Emperor Kanmu decided to relocate once more. And so, in 794, the capital was moved to Heian-kyō, kicking off a new era in Japan.

Art, Culture, and Literature during the Heian Period

The Heian period lasted for nearly four hundred years, and it was known as the last classical period in Japanese history while also being considered the turning point for the nation. Fine arts, culture, and literature were at their peak during this period. Most of the culture imported from the Asian mainland was, no doubt, vigorously infused to shape the Japanese culture, but when diplomatic missions to Tang China were forced to a halt in 894, Japan witnessed the birth of a new culture that contained little to zero influence from foreign lands.

Writing systems in Japan had been heavily influenced by the Chinese ever since the nation had started making contact with the Asian continent. Most documents were written in Chinese ideograms (kanji), but during the Heian period, the Japanese finally developed their very own script. Most of the Chinese characters were different from Japanese sounds. Although it was still based on Chinese characters, writers and priests worked together to create two Japanese writing systems. Consisting of approximately fifty characters, the two Japanese forms of writing or kana are known as katakana and hiragana; the latter is written in a cursive style.

Men preferred to use Chinese characters to create poems and various documents, although some of them did switch to using kana since it was simpler than kanji. Women would often produce their literature masterpieces using kana since few were familiar with kanji. This was due to a tradition where women would often be excluded from learning to write since they were not allowed to gain positions in the government. Nevertheless, the development of these two writing styles led to an increased number of literary works. Perhaps the most well-known piece of literature created in this period is the one by Murasaki Shikibu, a lady-in-waiting in the imperial court who had exceptional writing gifts. She was the author of *Genji Monogatari* or *The Tale of Genji*, the world's first novel. Consisting of fifty-four chapters, the novel tells the story of Genji, the son of an emperor. It includes the story of his love life as well as a great description of the lavish lifestyle of the aristocrats during the Heian period.

Yamato-e, a form of painting, originated during the Heian period. Simply translated as "Japanese painting," Yamato-e was often painted on scrolls, folding screens, and panels. This painting style involves vivid color schemes and depictions of the lives of nobles. The human figures in a Yamato-e painting appear small while its surrounding scenes are painted in great detail, combined with large bands of "floating clouds" covering the empty spaces or separating a scene. To depict multiple scenes in different spaces indoors, a technique called *fukinuki yatai* was used. Directly translated as "blown off roof," the technique involves painting a certain building or structure without its roof or using partitions to expose its interior and provide the viewer with an artistic perspective of a bird's eye view.

Image: A Yamato-e painting on folding screens.
https://commons.wikimedia.org/wiki/File:Soutatsu_Matsushima.jpg

A Yamato-e painting featuring the *fukinuki yatai* technique.
Metropolitan Museum of Art, CC0, via Wikimedia Commons:
https://commons.wikimedia.org/wiki/File:MET_2015_300_27ai_Burke_website.jpg

Architectural designs also blossomed during this period, especially when it came to palaces, estates, and mansions belonging to those of the elite class. Most of these structures were built based on a Japanese design called *shinden-zukuri*. The main features of this design include traditional Japanese blinds called *sudare*. It serves as a cover for an opening of a building from sunlight and rain. While it is typically made out of wood, palaces often use *sudare* made out of high-quality bamboo complete with silk and gold embroidery for decorative purposes. Some even feature a Yamato-e painting.

Shitomi, timber lattice shutters, were also common in the *shinden-zukuri* style, along with *tatami*, a type of flooring only found in mansions. The Heian Palace (modern-day Kyoto Imperial Palace) as well as the two Buddhist temples called Byōdō-in and Hōjō-ji, were some of the buildings that featured the *shinden-zukuri* design; the latter, however, was destroyed in a fire in 1053.

Traditional Japanese blinds, *sudare*, installed at the Kyoto Imperial Palace.
Wikiwikiyarou, CC BY-SA 4.0 https://creativecommons.org/licenses/by-sa/4.0 , via Wikimedia Commons: https://commons.wikimedia.org/wiki/File:Imperial_Throne_of_Shishinden_in_Kyoto_Imperial_Palace.jpg

Shitomi, traditional Japanese shutters.
Ktmchi, CC BY-SA 4.0 https://creativecommons.org/licenses/by-sa/4.0 , via Wikimedia Commons: https://commons.wikimedia.org/wiki/File:G321-HR07-09.jpg

The Life of the Common People in the Heian Period

By the middle of the Heian period, Japan's population had skyrocketed, reaching approximately six to seven million people. The capital alone was home to about a hundred thousand people, of which only a thousand or two belonged to the elite social class. While the aristocrats called the capital their home, the commoners still lived outside of the capital, where they mostly engaged in agricultural activities, especially rice farming. They lived in loose settlements instead of a crowded village, with houses placed at least a hundred meters away from each other. A house typically had around eight to ten people living in it at the same time.

Centuries after rice cultivation arrived in the Japanese archipelago, the farmers finally decided to change their rice farming methods. Instead of direct seeding, they started to become familiar with the transplanting method. Although the method had already been introduced to Japan way before the beginning of the Heian period, it was not entirely implemented since it seemed to be more complicated and time-consuming than direct seeding.

Farmers would start planting the seeds into a dry seedbed and wait for them to grow. Once the seeds turned into seedlings, the farmers had to take them out and transfer each one of them into a flooded field. Indeed, transferring one seedling at a time and making sure they were planted in neat and organized rows would take a lot of time and energy. However, this method guaranteed higher harvests since no weeds would disturb the growth of the rice. It also required more people, which explains why they lived in big groups.

This time-consuming rice farming process could also be the reason why newlyweds did not move into a new home and live together right away. Instead, they would continue living in their parents' house, and husbands would only visit their wives every once in a while at night. Children were also raised in the wife's household. For some couples, this situation would last their entire lifetime, although there most people would eventually leave their parents' house—typically after five or six years of marriage—and move in together.

Fashions of the Nobles and Elites

Clothing played an important part in identifying the nobles' rank in the imperial court. They dressed pretty much the same as those from the Nara period, but changes began to happen during the second half of the Heian period. *Jūnihitoe*, or the twelve-layered robe, was one of the garments popular during the era. It was worn only by the highest-ranking women in the imperial court. Despite its name, the wearer was not obliged to don exactly twelve layers of robes. In fact, the number of layers varied according to seasons, occasions, and ceremonies.

Jūnihitoe, the twelve-layered formal robe worn by high-ranking women during the Heian period.

The counterpart to the *jūnihitoe* was the *sokutai*. It was worn by elite men during formal events such as weddings and enthronement ceremonies. A *sokutai* has an outer robe (*ho*) and a black silk hat that was sometimes decorated with a chrysanthemum crest. The men would hold a flat ritual scepter called a *shaku*. Other garments worn by noblemen include *noshi* (everyday wear) and *kariginu* (hunting dress). The latter was also worn at Shinto and Buddhist rituals.

Sokutai, formalwear worn by high-ranking men during the Heian period.
https://commons.wikimedia.org/wiki/File:Tsukuba_Fujimaro.jpg

Dyeing techniques were also improved during this period, leading to an explosion of colors in fashion. While there were many color schemes, a specific dye named *kurenai* or scarlet was reserved only for women in the imperial line, while another dye called *aka* or red was restricted for men holding a certain rank in the court. The different colors in their clothing were aimed not only to portray their ranks but also their age, marital status, and reputation.

White skin was considered attractive for a woman in ancient Japan, so she would apply rice powder on both her face and neck.

To ease the process of applying the rice powder to their face, the nobles, especially women, would pluck or shave their natural eyebrows before drawing them slightly higher on the forehead using a type of powdered ink named *haizumi*. This practice of removing eyebrows is known as *hikimayu*. White teeth, however, were not a popular look back then. The Heian aristocrats were known for their pitch-black teeth. *Ohaguro* is an ancient Japanese custom that involves dyeing teeth black. This tradition was believed to have emerged during the Kofun period, but it was common among the Heian elites.

But despite the vibrant fashions and cosmetic looks, it was considered rude for men to look directly at a woman's face. Because of that, bamboo curtains hung from the ceiling, and painted fans were used to cover women from their sight. The only thing they could see was the edges of the women's sleeves.

Yamato State vs. the Emishi People

The Yamato court had long spread its power all over Japan except for the northeastern Honshu region, which was the home of the Emishi people. While the origins of the Emishi remain debatable, some suggest that they were descendants of the Jomon people, while others claim that they were related to the Ainu people. Nevertheless, these people strongly resisted the expansion of the Yamato state.

The Yamato often thought of the Emishi as barbarians and uncivilized people. It wished to expand its power and move toward an even more centralized state, which resulted in a conquest mission. Back in the Nara period, the central government had proclaimed its power over the region of northeastern Honshu by installing two provinces called Dewa and Mutsu in these lands. Later on, outposts were established in these regions in an attempt to assert their influence over the Emishi. Settlements were also built farther in the regions, and stockades defended by the government military began to appear. The Yamato state even went to the length of inviting the chiefs of the Emishi to the capital, where they absorbed them into the imperial court and gave them bureaucrat ranks. Some of them decided to migrate and join the state; those who were not convinced stayed behind.

However, as more settlements were built in the northeastern Honshu region, the Emishi people began to become irritated as the Yamato's attempt to invade their territories became clearer. And so, they began to sharpen their spears and arrows to get ready for a possible war. The Emishi people were divided into several tribes, and some of them even waged war against each other once in a while. But to push the Yamato forces back to their capital, these tribes were left with no choice but to unite. They began raiding the Yamato settlements scattered throughout their territories and killed the provincial government officials, leading to several small-scale wars with the Yamato court in the early 8th century CE.

The conflict between the imperial court and the Emishi tribes only became worse as time passed. Eventually, war was officially declared by the Yamato court in 774. The long, terrible conflict is known as the Thirty-Eight Years' War, and it undoubtedly caused heavy casualties on both sides. Victory, however, looked like it was siding with the Emishi people. They managed to burn down not only the villages of the Japanese but also Taga Castle, which was the imperial court's main base of operation in the north. In response, the imperial court recruited at least twenty thousand military forces to fend off the Emishi tribes, which only had three thousand warriors. An attack was launched against the Emishi in 776, but it ended terribly for the Japanese. Again, in 789, another battle ensued between the two factions; this one is known as the Battle of Koromo River. The Japanese forces were once again defeated by the Emishi tribe, which was led by a powerful general named Aterui.

However, a ray of light finally shone upon the imperial court when the Japanese forces welcomed a new skilled shogun general named Sakanoue no Tamuramaro into their long battle. The general launched another attack against the Emishi using well-trained horse archers. The relentless war eventually came to an end when Aterui was forced to surrender in 802, thus ending the long war between the imperial court and the Emishi people. After the victory, Sakanoue no Tamuramaro brought Aterui and his lieutenant back to the imperial capital as prisoners, where he suggested the emperor spare their lives. The shogun general claimed that their skills in war could be put to good use and benefit the government. The emperor was not pleased with the suggestion since the state had faced much destruction from the terrible war. So, instead of a royal pardon, Aterui and his loyal companion were executed. Although there was still slight resistance by the Emishi after the defeat of Aterui and his forces, the Yamato state successfully pushed its border farther to the north.

The Dominance of the Fujiwara Clan and the Establishment of a Cloistered Government

The Fujiwara clan was divided into four different houses; each one of them had been founded by the four sons of Fujiwara no Fuhito. These main houses were known as Nanke (Southern), Hokke (Northern), Shikike (Ceremonial), and Kyoke (Capital). But when Japan transitioned into the Heian period, the Hokke rose to power and eventually dominated the entire imperial court. They asserted their power by marrying Fujiwara women to the emperors. Fujiwara no Yoshifusa, for instance, married his daughter to Emperor Montoku (the fifty-fifth emperor of Japan). The two bore a son, who later became the emperor's crown prince.

When Emperor Montoku died in 858, his crown prince, who was only nine years old at the time, was enthroned as the new emperor. Since he was merely a child, Fujiwara no Yoshifusa grabbed the opportunity and made himself a regent or *sesshō*. He would govern the state on behalf of the young Emperor Seiwa. This was also the first time the position of regent was given to a person outside of the imperial line. Since a *sesshō* was only appointed to rule on behalf of a child emperor, they had to step down once the emperor came of age. The Fujiwara, however, was not planning to give their power away so easily. They established another title called *kampaku*, which is essentially a regent for adult emperors. Many in the court opposed the idea since it would mean that the emperor was no longer placed on top of the pyramid and only acted as a figurehead. But these oppositions were a waste of time. Both titles of *sesshō* and *kampaku* eventually became permanent and were only reserved for those belonging to the Hokke Fujiwara clan. This marked the dominance of the Fujiwara, and it lasted for the next two hundred years.

The clan's power soon began to wane when Emperor Go-Sanjō rose to the throne in 1068. Being the first emperor since the 9th century who was not born from a Fujiwara mother, he was indeed against the Fujiwara's dominance in the imperial court. He began to establish a couple of reforms and offices in hopes of curbing the clan's power. Four years later, the emperor abdicated the throne in favor of his son, Shirakawa, and went on to establish the office of the retired emperor (*In no chō*). The retired emperor planned to continue his efforts of erasing Fujiwara power by starting a cloistered rule—a form of government where retired emperors held the true power. But unfortunately, he passed away a few years later. His plan was then resumed by his own son, Emperor Shirakawa, who successfully set the cloistered rule system into motion, thus greatly weakening the dominance of the Fujiwara clan.

Minamoto and Taira Clans: The Origin of the Samurai

Although the Heian period was when the unique Japanese culture began to flourish, the government was surprisingly in the midst of financial difficulties. One of the reasons for these financial problems was the never-ending imperial line. The ancient emperors of Japan were well known for having a long list of children. Emperor Kanmu, for instance, had thirty-six children in total, while Emperor Saga had forty-nine. Each of the members of the royal family was given an allowance, which had seriously drained the royal coffers.

So, to solve the problem and save government funds, Emperor Kanmu began to demote many of his descendants; this method was also practiced by his successors. He removed at least a hundred of his descendants from the imperial house, gave them the title of nobles, and sent them to live in different provinces across the Japanese archipelago. These demoted imperial members were, of course, no longer in line for the throne, and they were also given new surnames: Minamoto and Taira. The latter was given to the grandchildren of Emperor Kanmu, while Taira was bestowed upon the descendants of Emperor Saga. Although these two clans started off as demoted members of the imperial family, they soon evolved into warriors. Today, we know them as samurai.

While the Taira clan remained in the shadows, the Minamoto clan first gained fame in the archipelago when the central government was in need of military forces on the field against the Abe clan in Mutsu Province. The Abe clan was initially tasked by the government to oversee the Emishi people and collect taxes from them. However, things got worse when the Abe started to take matters into their own hands. They stopped sending tax money to the central government and began causing trouble with the governor of Mutsu, which eventually led to violence in 1051.

The government appointed two powerful figures from the Minamoto clan to lead their troops against the rebellious Abe. Without delaying more time, Minamoto no Yoriyoshi and his son, Minamoto no Yoshiie, mounted their horses with bows and arrows at the ready and easily demolished the Abe clan. Minamoto no Yoshiie was known for his exceptional skills in archery and horseback riding. He had emerged victorious in dozens of battles to the point that he became the kami of the Minamoto clan. The Minamoto forged an alliance with the Fujiwara clan to remove anti-government rebels. Men from the Minamoto clan were regarded as being the greatest warriors in the Heian period.

The Minamoto clan's power, however, began to spiral out of control after the death of Yoshiie. Troubles arose when one of Yoshiie's sons, Minamoto no Yoshichika, started a rebellion against the government and violently murdered several government officials. Hoping to put the issue to rest, the imperial court hired the leader of the Taira clan named Taira no Masamori, who managed to execute Yoshichika and the other Minamoto rebels. From this point onward, the Taira clan began to gain more power, thus starting a long rivalry with the Minamoto clan.

Chapter 15 – Fudō Myō-ō and Amida

Esoteric Buddhism, also known as Tantric Buddhism, can be traced back to ancient India. In the 8th century CE, the teachings were spread to other parts of the world. It was brought to Tibet by the guru Padmasambhava, while China welcomed a few Tantric masters from India, which led to the establishment of Mi-tsung or the School of Secrets. Later on, in 804, the Japanese monk named Kukai set sail to Tang China, where he became a student of Hui Guo, a Chinese Mi-tsung teacher. After a couple of years in Tang China, where Kukai obtained knowledge and teachings passed down by Hui Guo, he finally returned to the Japanese archipelago. He greatly wished to spread the knowledge that he had just mastered. Although his lessons did not get much attention at first, it was believed that through his exquisite calligraphy skills, those in the imperial court and the emperor himself began to notice his teachings. Eventually, the emperor became his patron, and Japan saw the birth of Shingon, one of the major schools of Japanese Buddhism.

With the birth of a new school of Japanese Buddhism in the 9th century came a group of Buddhist deities known as the Myō-ō.

Corresponding to the Vidyaraja in Sanskrit, the Myō-ō were initially Hindu deities who were then absorbed into the pantheon of Esoteric Buddhism. Despite being considered protective Buddhist deities and messengers of Dainichi Nyorai, the supreme Buddha of Shingon Buddhism, the Myō-ō are often depicted with menacing appearances. They are believed to have the ability to fend off and frighten evil spirits and vanquish blind cravings. There are a total of five deities of the Myō-ō: Go Sansei, Dai Itoku, Gundari-yasha, Kongō-yasha, and the most prominent one, Fudō Myō-ō.

A seated statue of Fudō Myō-ō.
https://commons.wikimedia.org/wiki/File:Fudo_Myoo_Museum_Rietberg_RJP_21.jpg

Featuring ferocious and wrathful facial expressions complete with a piercing stare, Fudō Myō-ō, also known as the Immovable One, is a form of the Buddha Vairocana and is regarded as the central deity of the Myō-ō. Aside from his intimidating facial expression, Fudō Myō-ō is often pictured in various threatening postures while being accompanied by a burst of bright orange flames behind him. The flames signify a process of purification of the mind from material desires, and his fierce face not only scares off evil spirits but also frightens nonbelievers and leads them toward the teachings of the Buddha Vairocana. Fudō Myō-ō also carries a sword called a *hōken* in one of his hands, which he uses to cut through both ignorance and ugly delusions. In his left hand is a *kensaku*, a lasso that is used to capture and bind the evil spirits. The deity is also sometimes depicted with a pair of fangs; one fang faces upward while the other faces downward.

Statues of Fudō Myō-ō are often placed deep in the mountains, caves, or near cascading waterfalls. The temple in Kyoto, Kiyomizu-dera, is one of the many temples that houses a statue of Fudō Myō-ō. It is placed near Otowa-no-taki, a waterfall with three separate streams associated with love, success, and longevity. Visitors and believers are allowed to drink from the streams should they wish to be blessed with either of the attributes associated with each of the streams. However, it is important to choose only one stream, as drinking water from each of them at the same time is considered greedy—a behavior that a Buddhist must avoid at all times should they wish to obtain enlightenment.

To purge evil desires and bad karma and purify negative thoughts, a traditional ritual involving fire is often performed. Known as Goma Taki, this specific ritual is only practiced in the Shingon sect. Taking place in Gomado, the hall where a sculpture of Fudō Myō-ō is housed, the ritual is often performed by priests every morning or afternoon. The traditional ritual involves the burning of wooden plates containing various wishes and prayers inscribed on them. The flame signifies the Buddha's wisdom, while the burning itself symbolizes the destruction of both evil desires and bad karma.

As a protector of Buddhism, it is not a surprise that Fudō Myō-ō became an important deity for warriors, especially for the samurai. The samurai were said to have carried images of Fudō Myō-ō on the battlefield. Images of the fierce deity were placed on either their breastplates or helmets, as it could act as a protection for the vital organs in those areas.

A samurai armor plate featuring a depiction of Fudō Myō-ō.
Marshall Astor, CC BY-SA 2.0 https://creativecommons.org/licenses/by-sa/2.0 via Wikimedia Commons: https://commons.wikimedia.org/wiki/File:Hotoke_dou.jpg

Legend has it that the Japanese monk Kukai was once saved by Fudō Myō-ō. After mastering the teachings of Esoteric Buddhism in Tang China, the monk was preparing to embark on the long journey back to the Japanese archipelago. Sailing through an open sea is still not an easy task, as one must go through various weather systems. And a disastrous storm was in store for Kukai back in the 9th century. A heavy storm was believed to have caused a lot of trouble for the monk and the entire crew on board. An hour passed, then another, yet there was no sign of the storm subsiding any time soon. Instead, the wind was only getting stronger, and the ship continued to fight against the massive rolling waves.

Seeing that the weather was only getting worse by the minute, Kukai decided to turn to Fudō Myō-ō and began to pray. He prayed to the deity for protection; he wished for nothing but a safe return home so he could soon spread his teachings across the archipelago. Later on, the devout monk was said to have been bestowed with a vision. He saw the fierce deity ferociously cutting through the rolling waves that stood in the way, thus ending the storm completely. Perhaps Fudō Myō-ō did hear the monk's prayer after all, and thanks to him, Kukai and the rest of the crew on the ship could return to the land of the rising sun safe and sound.

Amida and Pure Land Buddhism

Amida Nyorai (referred to in Sanskrit as Amitabha Tathagata) is one of the most prominent Buddhist deities, especially in East Asia. Also known as the Buddha of Immeasurable Light, Amida, like Gautama Buddha, had also gone through a long journey before finally reaching enlightenment and entering the state of Buddhahood. The Infinite Life Sutra stated that Amida was once a king who went by the name of Dharmakara. He was believed to have renounced his throne and lifestyle when he came across the Buddhist teachings by Lokesvararaj, the fifty-fourth Buddha in history; he came long before Gautama Buddha. Impressed by his teachings, Dharmakara chose to live his life as a monk and focused on obtaining enlightenment.

After countless lives and reincarnations, Dharmakara finally accumulated enough merit to achieve enlightenment. Upon attaining Buddhahood, Dharmakara went on to create *Buddhasetra* ("Buddha Land"), a celestial land or paradise positioned in the west, beyond the boundaries of our world. He also took a total of forty-eight vows; for instance, the Buddha promised that he would grant anyone passage to his blissful land should they call upon his name. The Buddha even vowed that he and his two bodhisattvas would appear before those who had died while faithfully calling upon his name. The Buddha was also described as being gentle and accepting, which made him one of the most well-known Buddhist deities, especially in Japan when Pure Land Buddhism was established.

Buddhism was first introduced to the Japanese archipelago by the Kingdom of Baekje back in the 6th century CE. With Prince Shōtoku at the helm, the religion quickly flourished and was accepted by many, except, of course, for the Mononobe clan, which was strongly against it. However, the early forms of the religion that arrived in Japan at that time were mainly practices from Mahayana and Esoteric Buddhism, which mainly focused on the concept of universal salvation through an array of specific rituals. It was only by the mid-Heian period that the Japanese were more familiar with the practice of Pure Land Buddhism, which is notable for the spiritual field associated with the Buddha of Eternal Life, Amida.

The history of Pure Land Buddhism can be traced back to the 2nd century CE, when it was first developed in India. The teachings then continued to gain many new followers, especially in Kashmir and several other regions in Central Asia. By 147, Pure Land Buddhism made its way to China, where a Kushan Buddhist monk, Lokakṣema, translated the sutras into Chinese. In Japan, Pure Land Buddhism was introduced by a Tendai monk named Honen Shonin, who founded the Japanese Buddhist school called Jodo Shu (School of the Pure Land).

Buddhists sought only two things: to put an end to suffering and attain enlightenment. The journey to reach enlightenment is not an easy task, though. However, in Pure Land Buddhism, it is believed that one can effortlessly attain enlightenment by gaining entrance to Sukhavati ("Blissful Land"). But what exactly is Sukhavati, and how does one enter it?

According to the Pure Land sutras, Sukhavati, also known as the Pure Land of Amida Buddha, is a world that is filled with nothing but joy and pleasantness. The world was said to have trees growing with precious jewelry and golden bells hanging from them, while the surroundings are continuously accompanied by the soft tunes of birds chirping and whistling. At the center of the world, one could lay their eyes on Amida Buddha, who would probably be sitting calmly on a lotus floating in the middle of a terrace pond while being attended by two bodhisattvas: Avalokiteshvara and Mahasthamaprapta. Sukhavati is also where all wishes are made true. It is a place those who put their faith in Amida Buddha would enjoy before attaining enlightenment with ease.

To be reborn in the joyous world of Sukhavati, Honen taught his followers that they must practice *nembutsu*, a practice that involves chanting the name of Amida Buddha while putting absolute faith and trust in the deity. However, there is no specific way of chanting the name of the deity; it can be done alone or in groups, silently or aloud, and with or without prayer beads. Honen himself was said to have chanted Amida's name at least sixty thousand times a day. Through his teachings, the monk claimed that everyone could achieve salvation. The simplicity of *nembutsu* allowed aristocrats, devout monks, and those living in rural villages to take a step closer to enlightenment. Chanting the name of Amida Buddha did not require ultimate intelligence or proficiency; all that was needed was for a person to repeatedly chant "Namu Amida Buddha" ("Save me, O Amida Buddha").

While Honen received many new followers from various levels of Japan's social classes, his teachings also invited a few negative critics, especially from other Buddhist schools that had long been established on the archipelago. To add salt to the wound, two imperial ladies-in-waiting decided to convert to Honen's teachings. Elites were worried that Honen's teachings of Pure Land Buddhism might grow too influential and eventually surpass the influence of the other Buddhist schools, so Honen and his loyal followers were exiled in 1207. The monk, however, continued to spread his lessons to every single person he met—be they farmers, fishermen, peasants, or even prostitutes. He was eventually pardoned four years after his exile and allowed to return to the capital. A year after his return, Honen passed away. Some claimed that he passed away peacefully while chanting the name of Amida Buddha, thus allowing him to be reborn in the joyous world of Sukhavati. Despite the monk's death, Pure Land Buddhism continued to prosper and has become one of the most well-known Buddhist schools in Japan.

Chapter 16 – Preparing for the Age of the Samurai

The Heian period lasted for nearly four hundred years, and it saw the birth of many things. The Japanese writing systems were created in this era, leading to an explosion of literature masterpieces and arts. New architectural styles emerged that featured only a little influence from the Asian continent, and new Buddhist schools were established by monks who had returned from China, which resulted in the construction of many temples. The central government had faced several major changes as well. After engaging in wars with the Emishi people, the Yamato government succeeded in expanding its power to the north. Later on, the Fujiwara clan rose to even more power, which allowed them to hold the imperial court firmly in their hands. Two centuries later, though, the power in the court shifted again with the establishment of cloistered rule. The conflicts did not stop there, as the Heian period was also when the samurai began to emerge from the shadows and take their first steps to transform the state into a shogunate (a military dictatorship).

Hōgen Disturbance

Emperor Toba, the seventy-fourth emperor of Japan, was only four years old when he first rose to the Chrysanthemum Throne.

Under a cloistered government, the emperor was merely a figurehead; the real power was held by his grandfather, the retired Emperor Shirakawa. Soon, the retired emperor married Emperor Toba off to Fujiwara no Tamako, who later bore a child named Sutoku. Continuing the tradition of enthroning a young emperor in the court, Shirakawa forced his grandson, who had just turned twenty years old, into abdicating the throne in favor of his infant son Sutoku.

However, there are sources that claim Emperor Toba was not fond of his eldest son, the young Emperor Sutoku. This was due to a rumor saying that Sutoku's real father was, in fact, Emperor Shirakawa. Although it remains unsure whether or not the rumor is true, the retired Emperor Toba surely seemed to have bought it since he began to treat Sutoku coldly.

When Emperor Shirakawa passed away in 1129, six years after Sutoku's ascension to the throne, the retired Emperor Toba was finally able to step out of his grandfather's shadow and assert his political power. He forced Emperor Sutoku to step down. The young emperor complied, although he was unsatisfied with the decision. Toba placed Emperor Konoe, another one of his sons, on the throne. Unfortunately, Konoe was a sickly man, and he died of a disease thirteen years after his succession. There was another vacancy on the throne, and Sutoku hoped his son would rise as an emperor. However, much to his disappointment, the retired Emperor Toba enthroned Emperor Go-Shirakawa, another one of his sons with Fujiwara no Tamako. Realizing that it was becoming impossible for his heir to sit on the Chrysanthemum Throne, Sutoku decided to take action, which resulted in a serious dispute with the current emperor, Go-Shirakawa.

Upon noticing the heightened dispute between the retired Emperor Sutoku and the current Emperor Go-Shirakawa, the Fujiwara clan decided to become involved in the issue, hoping it could be a stepping stone for them to reinsert their power into the imperial court. However, two of the most powerful members of the Fujiwara clan, Fujiwara no Tadamichi and Fujiwara no Yorinaga, were not on good terms. The latter supported Sutoku, while his brother, Tadamichi, sided with Emperor Go-Shirakawa. To prepare for battle, the two factions (Sutoku and Go-Shirakawa) turned to the two most powerful samurai clans: Minamoto and Taira. Minamoto no Tameyoshi, the leader of the Minamoto clan, was quick to announce his support for the retired emperor and Fujiwara no Yorinaga. To raise enough troops for the upcoming battle, Tameyoshi tasked his own son, Minamoto no Yoshitomo, with traveling across the archipelago and enlisting as many warriors as possible. Yoshitomo succeeded in building a massive army, but he did not present them to his father. Yoshitomo instead abandoned his father and swore his bow to Emperor Go-Shirakawa and Fujiwara no Tadamichi.

Something similar happened to the Taira clan. The leader, Taira no Kiyomori, chose to support Go-Shirakawa, while his uncle, Taira no Tadamasa, sided with Sutoku. The dispute over the imperial throne reached its peak when Emperor Toba died in 1156 due to an unknown sickness. Legend has it that the retired emperor met his fate after he was cursed by his favorite courtesan, Tamamo-no-Mae, who was later revealed to be none other than the famous yōkai, the nine-tailed fox.

Those who had allied with Sutoku gathered at his palace, while Go-Shirakawa's loyal supporters and his massive samurai troop raised a defense within another palace nearby. When it was time to discuss a strategy for the battle, Minamoto no Tameyoshi suggested that they lay a surprise attack on Go-Shirakawa's palace at night. Although their forces were smaller than Go-Shirakawa's, Tameyoshi was confident with the plan since he had his other son, Minamoto no Tametomo, by his side. Tametomo was described as a legendary archer. Some claimed that he was able to sink a whole ship with only a single arrow and that his left arm was slightly longer than his right, allowing him to draw his bow better than any average archer.

However, Fujiwara no Yorinaga was against Tameyoshi's war strategy. He claimed that the only honorable way to defeat their enemies was to attack head-on instead of deploying a surprise attack when the skies were dark. Many agreed with Yorinaga's plan to hold their positions and wait for their enemies to arrive so that they could fight each other in a fair battle. Unfortunately, his plans were immediately foiled. Go-Shirakawa's forces laid a surprise attack at night. They charged toward Sutoku's palace gates, and a chaotic battle ensued.

The legendary archer, Minamoto no Tametomo, led his troops to defend the palace. On horseback, he began firing arrows at his opponents. The victory looked as if it belonged to Sutoku's forces at the beginning of the battle; however, everything spiraled out of control when an arrow lethally struck Fujiwara no Yorinaga, which soon resulted in his death. This was followed by the torching of Sutoku's palace. After witnessing the huge flames rapidly devouring every inch of the palace gates, Tametomo, Sutoku, and his remaining allies were forced to flee.

Emperor Go-Shirakawa emerged victorious, and it was not long until his rivals faced their fates. The ambitious retired emperor, Sutoku, was exiled; he died soon after. Some believed that he died unpleasantly, turning into an evil spirit that wished nothing but only misfortune upon those who wronged him. Minamoto no Tametomo, on the other hand, had the tendons in his left arm severed so that he could no longer fire an arrow precisely. He was then banished to an isolated location. His honor was severely tarnished, and he had lost his skills. The legendary archer slashed his own abdomen, committing the first seppuku (ritual suicide) in history.

The remaining allies of Sutoku were sentenced to death; however, Minamoto no Yoshitomo pleaded to the emperor to spare his father, Minamoto no Tameyoshi. Seeing all the destruction caused by the short civil war and not wanting to risk a situation where his enemy could regain his power, Emperor Go-Shirakawa showed no mercy. Yoshitomo had no other choice but to execute his father. The same thing happened to Taira no Kiyomori, who was forced to end his uncle's life.

With the rebellion a failure, the Japanese government remained under the rule of the retired emperor. Go-Shirakawa stepped down from the throne three years after his reign, but he remained in power behind the scene while his eldest son, Emperor Nijō, sat on the Chrysanthemum Throne. As a reward for their service and loyalty, Minamoto no Yoshitomo and Taira no Kiyomori were given promotions. However, their new ranks within the imperial court were not equal. The imperial house seemed to have favored the Taira over the Minamoto. And so, a bitter rivalry between the two samurai clans continued for years to come.

Four years after the Hōgen Disturbance came another bloody rebellion spearheaded by Minamoto no Yoshitomo, who had sealed an alliance with Fujiwara no Nobuyori. Upon receiving news that the head of the Taira clan, Taira no Kiyomori, and some other supporters of the imperial family were about to depart from Heian-kyō (Kyoto) for a religious pilgrimage, Yoshitomo began plotting. Yoshitomo and Nobuyori raised an army—approximately five hundred men strong—and marched toward the Sanjō Palace. There, the samurai kidnapped the retired Emperor Go-Shirakawa and his son, Emperor Nijō, before setting the palace on fire. Their next target was Go-Shirakawa's loyal supporter Fujiwara no Michinori, who had already made his escape earlier to the mountains near the capital. Unfortunately, it did not take long for the rebels to trace him. He was decapitated shortly after.

A painting of the night attack on Sanjō Palace.
https://commons.wikimedia.org/wiki/File:Heiji_Monogatari_Emaki_-
_Sanjo_scroll_part_5_-_v2.jpg

Manors and estates were set aflame. The screams could be heard from far away, and much blood was spilled. No one saw any semblance of peace for at least two weeks. Soon, Taira no Kiyomori returned to the chaotic capital. He and his son, Taira no Shigemori, managed to rescue Go-Shirakawa and his son, Emperor Nijō, from the Minamotos' grasp. A battle ensued between the two samurai clans later on, and the Minamoto clan was again defeated. Yoshitomo managed to escape to Owari Province, where he found refuge in the residence of Tadamune Osada, his retainer. But Yoshitomo's journey ended there, as he was eventually betrayed by his own retainer and murdered while he was bathing. Three of Yoshitomo's sons, Yoritomo, Noriyori, and Yoshitsune, were spared and banished.

Taira no Kiyomori had not only successfully strengthened his clan's position as the strongest and most powerful warrior clan in the entire Japanese archipelago, but he had also proved to be a master politician. Through the former emperor, Go-Shirakawa, Kiyomori managed to rise through the ranks and hold the title of chancellor (Daijō-daijin). He married his daughter into the imperial family, appointed those from the Taira clan as provincial governors, and gathered many Japanese to serve under his rule. Taira no

Kiyomori's power soon began to overshadow the retired Emperor Go-Shirakawa.

By 1180, Kiyomori installed his two-year-old grandson, Antoku, on the Chrysanthemum Throne. Prince Mochihito, the son of the former Emperor Go-Shirakawa, was enraged by this decision, especially since his opportunity to step up as emperor had been snatched away by an infant. The prince soon discovered that Taira's sudden domination over the central government had irritated many Japanese throughout the archipelago, especially those from the Minamoto clan and some other Buddhist warrior monks who had been wronged by Kiyomori the past few years. And so, Prince Mochihito put up a call to arms for anyone who was against the Taira. This marked the very beginning of the famous Genpei War, which lasted for five years.

The Genpei War

The first figure to answer Prince Mochihito's call to arms was none other than Minamoto no Yorimasa. The first battle of the Genpei War took place in Uji. When word about Prince Mochihito's plot to overthrow the Taira reached Kiyomori, he sent his troops to demolish the rebels. The prince, Yorimasa, and his few troops were left with no choice but to retreat to Mii-dera, a Buddhist temple located at the foot of Mount Hiei. Realizing that they arrived too late to defend the temple, the Minamoto troops, Prince Mochihito, and several remaining Buddhist warrior monks fought their way to Byōdō-in, another Buddhist temple in Uji.

An illustration of the Battle of Uji.
https://commons.wikimedia.org/wiki/File:Ukiyo-e_War.jpg

Right after crossing the Uji River, the Minamoto clan immediately destroyed the bridge behind them, hoping that the pursuing Taira clan would not be able to reach them. The Taira troops remained insistent on their goal of defeating the Minamoto, and they were said to have crossed the river on their horses. Accepting that defeat was around the corner, Prince Mochihito attempted an escape, but it was not to be; he was captured and executed. Minamoto no Yorimasa, on the other hand, retreated behind the walls of Byōdō-in and committed seppuku. It is believed that after Yorimasa let out his last breath, one of his loyal followers unsheathed his blade and cut off Yorimasa's head. He tied his lord's severed head to a stone and threw it into the river. This was done to ensure that his lord's head would never become a trophy for the Taira.

The Taira emerged victorious yet again after defeating Yorimasa and his samurai troops. But this incident was only the beginning of the terrible war. The Taira victory eventually drew the attention of Minamoto no Yoritomo and his brothers, Noriyori and Yoshitsune—these were the banished sons of Minamoto no Yoshitomo who had grown up over the years and were ready to cleanse their tarnished clan's name. Not long after the Battle of Uji, Kiyomori witnessed the rise of many rebels throughout the Japanese provinces. It turns out that the Taira clan, despite its growing power, had made a lot of enemies.

Minamoto no Yoritomo had witnessed his father's murder and was expecting to be executed by the Taira clan. But somehow, Kiyomori decided to show mercy and spared the thirteen-year-old boy and his two brothers; some claimed that he only spared them due to his stepmother's request. And so, Yoritomo was exiled and sent to Izu Province, where he was raised and cared for by the Hōjō clan, another branch of the Taira clan. Yoritomo stayed in the shadows for nearly twenty years, and he even married the daughter of the Hōjō clan's leader. Thinking that the boy was no longer a threat, Kiyomori let out a sigh of relief since he did not have to keep his eyes on him anymore. This was a mistake that he would soon regret.

The terrible aftermath of the Battle of Uji fed Yoritomo's anger, and he sought to overthrow the Taira once and for all. Supported by the Hōjō clan, Yoritomo gathered allies from the warriors of Izu Province and raised his own samurai army. Noriyori and Yoshitsune, who had been exiled to different parts of Japan, joined forces and supported their brother's mission. Soon after, Yoritomo bravely declared war against the ruling Taira.

The first small-scale battle ensued; however, Yoritomo's forces faced their first defeat. After Yoritomo was forced to retreat, he came up with another plan; he would establish an independent warrior state in the Kanto region. Back then, the Kanto region was full of skilled warriors who harbored deep hatred toward the unfair central government. Even the first known samurai, Taira no Masakado, once attempted to remove the central government from the region. Promising the warriors of the Kanto region land and freedom under his rule, Yoritomo gradually earned enough support to the point where he managed to establish a base in Kamakura. His next move was to remove the government headquarters scattered throughout the region. Those who had supported the Taira clan began to see his potential, and many of them switched sides and became loyal followers of the rising leader of the Minamoto clan. In just a short span of time, Yoritomo had successfully conquered the region. He welcomed those who chose to support him and annihilated those who strongly opposed him.

The Taira was well aware of Yoritomo's growing power, but due to an unfortunate famine taking over the lands of Japan, they were forced to delay their attack. When the time finally came, the Taira troops marched toward Fujikawa to face Yoritomo's forces. The Taira samurai soon realized they were heavily outnumbered, and they immediately retreated. Legend has it that the Taira began to doubt their victory once they noticed dozens of fires emerging from the darkness. They assumed that the fires were from the Minamoto camps when it was, in fact, cooking fires lit by peasants who were taking shelter from the upcoming war. The Tairas' fear grew even stronger when they were startled by the thunderous sound of a flock of birds suddenly flying in the skies. The Taira thought it was the Minamoto galloping on their horses to lay a surprise attack on them. And so, many of them left their campsites and retreated back to the capital.

With the retreat of the Taira army, Yoritomo shifted his focus back to his base in the Kanto region. While he worked on solidifying his position, conquest missions and battles were left to Kiso Yoshinaka, who is also known as Lord Kiso. According to *Heike Monogatari* (*The Tale of the Heike*), a compilation of events during the clash of the two samurai clans, Lord Kiso had a powerful supporter by his side. She was known by the name Tomoe Gozen, and she served under Lord Kiso as an onna-musha or a female warrior specially trained in martial arts and combat. Aside from her extreme beauty, Tomoe was said to possess exceptional skills in archery, sword fighting, and horseback riding. She was often appointed as the lord's first captain or commander. Tomoe would often ride to war wearing full armor and was equipped with a bow and an oversized sword that she would use to decapitate her enemies.

With Tomoe by his side, Lord Kiso launched several attacks against the samurai troops from the Taira clan and expanded his influence across much of the archipelago. His name soon echoed throughout the capital, and the Taira began to take notice.

An illustration of Tomoe Gozen in battle.
https://commons.wikimedia.org/wiki/File:Battle_of_Awazugahara.jpg

The Taira, on the other hand, had lost their leader, Taira no Kiyomori, to a serious fever in 1181. Honoring his father's wish, Taira no Munemori became the clan's leader, while his brother, Taira no Tomomori, served as the chief commander for the war. Under this new leadership, the Taira enjoyed victory after victory against the Minamoto in a couple of battles. Buddhist temples, such as Tōdai-ji, Mii-dera, and Kōfuku-ji, were burned since the monks supported the Minamoto clan. Their victory, however, did not last long, especially once the retired emperor, Go-Shirakawa, defected to the Minamotos. There was also an invasion of the capital led by Lord Kiso.

The ongoing war between the two warrior clans was paused when the archipelago was plagued by horrible disasters. First, there was a typhoon, and then came extreme famine. The people were desperate, and it wasn't just the peasants who were suffering. Death was nearly everywhere, and bodies lined the streets. Those who were still breathing decided to move to the mountains in hopes of saving their lives. There, they could live off of fishing and hunting. The elites began trading their valuables for food supplies, although few would give up their food in exchange for shiny jewelry during this unfortunate time.

The war eventually resumed in 1183 when the famine finally subsided. The Taira launched an attack on Lord Kiso, who eventually lured them into a narrow valley called Jigokudani. Lord Kiso's troops managed to surround the Taira, and they clashed swords and fired arrows at one another. Legends even claim that Lord Kiso annihilated the Taira by using oxen. The lord was said to have gathered a herd of oxen nearby and tied burning torches on their heads before causing a stampede into the Taira army. How true this story is remains unsure, but we do know that Lord Kiso successfully defeated the Taira army, thus opening an opportunity for him to march toward the capital.

After the Taira received the news that Lord Kiso and his samurai army were en route to the capital, they donned their armor and began searching for more allies to support them. They even turned to the Buddhist monks for support, but they all refused to support them due to the burning and destruction of their temples. The Taira, knowing that they were outnumbered, decided to flee from the capital. They brought the young emperor, Antoku, and three of the imperial regalia—the Kusanagi sword, the jewel named Yasakani no Magatama, and the sacred mirror called Yata no Kagami—with them.

In the absence of the Taira and the young emperor, Lord Kiso could freely wander around the capital without having to worry about getting attacked. However, there was only room for one leader in the Minamoto clan. Lord Kiso's growing power worried Minamoto no Yoritomo. So, Yoritomo forged an alliance with the former emperor, Go-Shirakawa, who was not at all fond of Lord Kiso and the terror that he had brought to the capital. To suppress Lord Kiso's power entirely, Yoritomo sent his two brothers,

Yoshitsune and Noriyori, to the capital. This resulted in the Battle of Awazu. Lord Kiso and his most loyal followers perished.

Through Go-Shirakawa, Kamakura was recognized as a military state. The court then issued an order to demolish the entire Taira clan, most of whom had fled the capital, along with the young emperor. Without sparing a moment, Yoritomo sent his brothers to destroy the Tairas' remaining posts and attack their base. The long rivalry between the two clans reached its peak during the naval Battle of Dan-no-ura, which took place in the Strait of Shimonoseki.

An illustration of the naval Battle of Dan-no-ura.
https://commons.wikimedia.org/wiki/File:AntokuTennou_Engi.7%268_Dannoura_Kassen.jpg

The Taira was well known for their exceptional seafaring skills. However, they were far outnumbered by the Minamoto—the Taira only had about 500 ships, while the Minamoto, under the command of Yoshitsune, had nearly 840 ships. Realizing that the Minamoto clan was quickly gaining the upper hand in the battle, one of the Taira generals named Taguchi Shigeyoshi decided to betray his own clan. He managed to turn his men against the Taira lords and swear their bows to the Minamoto instead. The Taira faced a terrible defeat at Dan-no0ura. The clan's leader, Taira no Munemori, was executed. The chief commander Tomomori committed suicide by tying an anchor to his feet and leaping into the deep sea. The grandmother of the young Emperor Antoku took him in her arms and leaped into the sea as well, where they drowned.

The ruling Taira clan was no more, and the Minamoto finally emerged victorious. This ended the Heian period and kicked off a whole new era: the Kamakura period. Following the war, Yoritomo established the very first shogunate, a military government that dominated the Japanese archipelago for centuries.

Conclusion

Japan has come a long way. Ten thousand years ago, the nation was only a chain of islands filled with rich nature and hunter-gatherers who lived in simple tents made entirely out of animal skins. As the centuries went by, these prehistoric inhabitants of Japan began to evolve as new technologies were introduced. From foraging forests and hunting boars, they focused on plant cultivation, especially rice. More ritualistic ceremonies took place, and later on, Shinto beliefs were established. Dozens of clans and tribes emerged, with each of them showcasing their power over the many regions of Japan. Wars exploded, and bloodshed became the norm. Then, the first line of the imperial family was born. They strived to unite the entire archipelago under a centralized government, an effort that took many centuries to come to fruition.

Many might agree that China and Korea played an important role in Japan's development. The art, culture, and even religious beliefs were heavily influenced by the Asian mainland. For instance, Buddhism came to Japan via one of the three ancient Korean kingdoms, the imperial capitals were constructed mainly using the Chinese grid system, constitutions and laws were created based on Buddhism doctrines combined with Confucian beliefs, and even *biwa*, a traditional Japanese lute, was influenced by the Chinese musical instrument called *pipa*. However, despite all of the influences that arrived on the archipelago, Japan was not subjected to foreign political control. The people were free to choose what foreign ideas they should adapt and infuse into their traditions and beliefs, thus creating cultures and customs unique to the country.

Today, Japan is considered to be one of the most advanced countries in the world. Despite all the complex new technologies and modern lifestyles, the Japanese are still deeply connected to their ancient roots. The busy metropolitan city of Tokyo might be packed with endless modern structures, skyscrapers, towers, and shopping complexes with neon lights lighting up during nighttime. But traditional houses with *tatami* floorings, *shoji* (the traditional Japanese sliding door), and *sudare* (traditional Japanese window coverings) are not an uncommon sight. Many Buddhist temples dated from the ancient periods are still intact today, and the existence of over 100,000 Shinto shrines across the archipelago tells us that the ancient religion has not been forgotten; in fact, Buddhism and Shintoism continue to peacefully coexist to the point that it is common for someone to practice both beliefs and ritualistic rituals. Kimonos, traditional Japanese clothing that originated from the Heian period, are still widely used by the Japanese, as are geta, a pair of wooden clogs typically worn with the traditional Japanese socks called tabi.

Important events that took place during ancient times are recalled in the forms of theatrical performances, traditional dances, and songs to ensure the efforts of their ancestors are never forgotten. All of those incidents, battles, and conflicts definitely paved the way for Japan to become what it is today. Starting off only as a small kingdom isolated from the Asian mainland, Japan is now known as one of the most influential countries in the whole world. Its colorful history, traditions, and culture are known by many. More movies, books, artwork, and even video games have adopted stories of Japan's ancient past. Because of this, Japan's ancient history has been kept alive within its people, and it has also been forever immortalized among those outside of the archipelago. To put it in simple words, the history of ancient Japan is unlikely to ever disappear.

Here's another book by Enthralling History that you might like

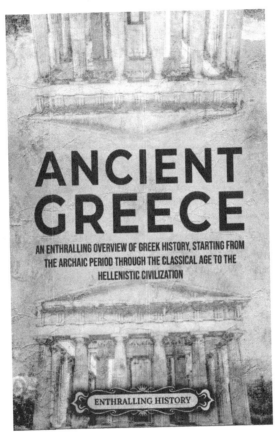

Free limited time bonus

Stop for a moment. We have a free bonus set up for you. The problem is this: we forget 90% of everything that we read after 7 days. Crazy fact, right? Here's the solution: we've created a printable, 1-page pdf summary for this book that you're reading now. All you have to do to get your free pdf summary is to go to the following website: **https://livetolearn.lpages.co/enthrallinghistory/**

Once you do, it will be intuitive. Enjoy, and thank you!

Bibliography

An Overview of Shintoism and Buddhism in Japan – Differences and History. (2021, September 30). Japan Wonder Travel Blog. https://blog.japanwondertravel.com/an-overview-of-shintoism-and-buddhism-in-japan-differences-and-history-20672

Armstrong, K. (2022, January 5). *History of Kimono: Classical Japan (Nara and Heian Periods).* Owlcation. https://owlcation.com/humanities/History-of-Kimono-Part-2-Nara-and-Heian-Periods

Buddhism: Pure Land Buddhism. (n.d.). BBC. Retrieved October 2, 2002, from

https://www.bbc.co.uk/religion/religions/buddhism/subdivisions/pureland_1.shtml

Cartwright, M. (2022, April 8). *Amaterasu.* World History Encyclopedia.

https://www.worldhistory.org/Amaterasu

Cartwright, M. (2022, April 8). *Heian Period.* World History Encyclopedia.

https://www.worldhistory.org/Heian_Period

Cartwright, M. (2022, April 9). *Fujiwara Clan*. World History Encyclopedia.

https://www.worldhistory.org/Fujiwara_Clan

Cartwright, M. (2022, April 9). *Genpei War*. World History Encyclopedia.

https://www.worldhistory.org/Genpei_War

Cartwright, M. (2022, April 9). *Kofun*. World History Encyclopedia.

https://www.worldhistory.org/Kofun

Cartwright, M. (2022, April 10). *Minamoto Clan*. World History Encyclopedia.

https://www.worldhistory.org/Minamoto_Clan

Cartwright, M. (2022, April 11). *Asuka Period*. World History Encyclopedia.

https://www.worldhistory.org/Asuka_Period

Cartwright, M. (2022, April 11). *Buddhism in Ancient Japan*. World History Encyclopedia.

https://www.worldhistory.org/article/1080/buddhism-in-ancient-japan

Cartwright, M. (2022, April 11). *Haniwa*. World History Encyclopedia.

https://www.worldhistory.org/Haniwa

Cartwright, M. (2022, April 11). *Izanami and Izanagi*. World History Encyclopedia.

https://www.worldhistory.org/Izanami_and_Izanagi

Cartwright, M. (2022, April 11). *Queen Himiko*. World History Encyclopedia.

https://www.worldhistory.org/Queen_Himiko

Chakra, H. (2021, April 17). *Yamato Clan and State, The Birthplace of the Japanese Political State. About History.* https://about-history.com/yamato-clan-and-state-the-birthplace-of-the-japanese-political-state/?amp

D. (2016, January 1). *The Controversial Iwajuku Site and the Argument for the Japanese Paleolithic Period. Ancient Origins.* https://www.ancient-origins.net/ancient-places-asia/controversial-iwajuku-site-and-argument-japanese-paleolithic-period-005081

Fudo Myo-o (Fudou Myou-ou) - Wrathful Messenger Who Protects & Serves Dainichi Buddha, Japanese Buddhism Art History. (n.d.). Copyright 1995 Onmark Productions.Com. All Right Reserved. https://www.onmarkproductions.com/html/fudo.html

Goma Fire Ritual. (n.d.). Seattle Koyasan. https://seattlekoyasan.com/services/goma-fire-ritual

The Great Buddha Hall. (n.d.). The Tōdai-ji. http://www.todaiji.or.jp/english/map02.html

Great South Gate (Nandai-mon). (n.d.). Tōdai-ji. http://www.todaiji.or.jp/english/map01.html

H. (2013, March 5). *Shoso-in Exhibition Treasures.* Heritage of Japan. https://heritageofjapan.wordpress.com/2011/09/22/shoso-in-exhibition-treasures/amp

Haniwa Tomb Figure of a Soldier. (n.d.). Wellesley College. https://www.wellesley.edu/davismuseum/artwork/node/36990

Hays, J. (n.d.). *JOMON PEOPLE (10,500–300 B.C.): RELIGION AND BURIAL CUSTOMS.* Facts and Details. https://factsanddetails.com/japan/cat16/sub105/entry-5607.html

Hays, J. (n.d.). *JOMON PERIOD (10,500–300 B.C.).* Facts and Details.

https://factsanddetails.com/japan/cat16/sub105/item2764.html#chapter-3

Hays, J. (n.d.). *ORIGIN OF THE YAYOI PEOPLE (AND MODERN JAPANESE)*. Facts and Details. https://factsanddetails.com/japan/cat16/sub105/entry-5284.html

Hays, J. (n.d.). *WA AND EARLY CONTACTS BETWEEN CHINA AND JAPAN*. Facts and Details. https://factsanddetails.com/japan/cat16/sub105/entry-5289.html#chapter-6

Hays, J. (n.d.). *WRITING AND LITERATURE IN THE HEIAN PERIOD (794–1185)*. Facts and Details. https://factsanddetails.com/japan/cat16/sub106/entry-5313.html#chapter-5

History of Japan: Heian Period (794–1185). (2021, September 30). Japan Wonder Travel Blog. https://blog.japanwondertravel.com/history-of-japan-heian-period-24207#toc4

HimikoHistory.com Editors. (2021, September 15). *Buddhism*. HISTORY. https://www.history.com/.amp/topics/religion/buddhism

Hoang, T. (2022, April 11). *Jomon Period*. World History Encyclopedia.

https://www.worldhistory.org/Jomon_Period/Japanese Amida Buddha

K. (2020, March 18). *Hashihaka Kofun and Japan's Beginnings*. Kansai Odyssey.

http://kansai-odyssey.com/hashihaka-kofun-and-japans-beginnings

K., & K. (2018, May 13). *The Isshi Incident*. Samurai World. https://samurai-world.com/the-isshi-incident

Kayashima: The Japanese Train Station Built Around a 700-Year-Old Tree. (2018, January

17). Colossal. https://www.thisiscolossal.com/2017/01/kayashima-the-japanese-train-station-built-around-a-700-year-old-tree

Kessler, P. L. (n.d.). *Early Japanese Cultures*. The History Files. https://www.historyfiles.co.uk/KingListsFarEast/JapanCultures.htm

Lane, V. (2015, June 17). *Jigoku and Yomi No Kuni: Exploring Japanese Hell*. Tofugu. https://www.tofugu.com/japan/japanese-hells

Lisina, E. (2021, December 13). *Fudo Myo.* JapanTravel. https://en.japantravel.com/blog/fudo-myo/68296

M. (2020, May 21). *Hōsōgami*. Yokai.Com. https://yokai.com/housougami

Mason, R. H. P., & Caiger, J. G. (1997). *A History of Japan: Revised Edition* (Revised ed.). Tuttle Publishing.

National Geographic Society. (2012, October 9). *Continental Drift*. https://www.nationalgeographic.org/encyclopedia/continental-drift

National Geographic Society. (2020, July 7). *Buddhism* https://www.nationalgeographic.org/encyclopedia/buddhism

Power of Plate Tectonics: Pangaea. (n.d.). American Museum of Natural History. https://www.amnh.org/explore/ology/earth/power-of-plate-tectonics/pangaea

S. (2020, January 20). *Naumann Elephant and Lake Nojiri*. Official Travel Guide of Shinanomachi, Nagano. http://shinanomachi-nagano.jp/en/wp/?p=281

Shingon - Japanese Esoteric Buddhism. (2017, March 6). Learn Religions. https://www.learnreligions.com/shingon-449632

Shinto. (2022, March 22). Japan-Guide.Com. https://www.japan-guide.com/e/e2056.html

Thomson, D. J. (2020, December 29). *Ise Grand Shrine: Everything You Need to Know about Japan's Most Sacret Shinto Shrine*. JRPass.Com. https://www.jrpass.com/blog/ise-grand-shrine-everything-you-need-to-know-about-japans-most-sacret-shinto-shrine

Who is Amida Buddha? - Buddhism for Beginners. (2020, April 25). Buddhism for Beginners.
https://tricycle.org/beginners/buddhism/who-is-amida-buddha

Wikipedia contributors. (2021, December 18). *Battle of Uji (1180)*. Wikipedia

https://en.wikipedia.org/wiki/Battle_of_Uji_(1180)

Wikipedia contributors. (2022, March 23). *Geology of Japan*. Wikipedia

https://en.m.wikipedia.org/wiki/Geology_of_Japan

Wikipedia contributors. (2022, March 23). *Tomoe Gozen*. Wikipedia

https://en.wikipedia.org/wiki/Tomoe_Gozen

Won, J. (2022, March 30). *An Ancient Battle Where Japan Fought for Korean Independence*. Medium.
https://historyofyesterday.com/an-ancient-battle-where-japan-fought-for-korean-independence-436590117e19

Wright, G. (2021, November 19). *Ebisu*. Mythopedia.
https://mythopedia.com/topics/ebisu

Yasuka, A. (2021, February 3). *Empress Suiko: The First Empress Regnant of Japan*. KCP International.
https://www.kcpinternational.com/2015/12/empress-suiko-the-first-empress-regnant-of-japan

Yayoi linked to Yangtze area: DNA tests reveal similarities to early wet-rice farmers. (2008, July 2). Heritage of Japan.
https://heritageofjapan.wordpress.com/yayoi-era-yields-up-rice/who-were-the-yayoi-people/yayoi-linked-to-yangtze-area-dna-tests-reveal-similarities-to-early-wet-rice-farmers

Made in the USA
Coppell, TX
27 December 2023

26940643R00108